T0082170

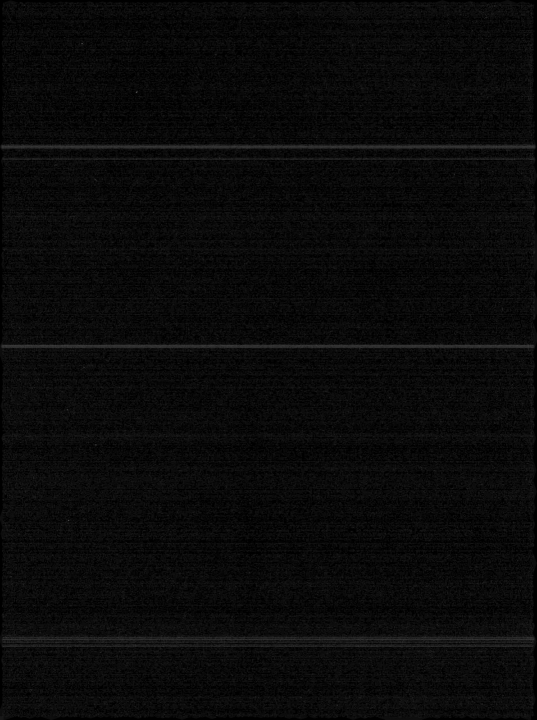

CONCEALED WORDS

숨겨둔 말

Concealed Words

by Sin Yong-Mok

Translated by Brother Anthony of Taizé

Black Ocean
Boston · Chicago

Copyright © 2017 by Sin Yong-Mok
Copyright © 2022 by Sin Yong-Mok
Copyright © 2022 by Brother Anthony of Taizé.
All rights reserved.

누군가 누군가를 부르면 내가 돌아보았다
Originally published in Korea by Changbi Publishers, Inc.
English edition is published by arrangement with
Changbi Publishers, Inc.

To reprint, reproduce, or transmit electronically, or by recording all or
part of this manuscript, beyond brief reviews or educational purposes,
please send a written request to the publisher at:

Black Ocean
P.O. Box 52030
Boston, MA 02205
blackocean.org

Cover Art and Design by Abby Haddican | abbyhaddican.com
Book Design by Taylor D. Waring | taylordwaring.com

ISBN: 978-1-939568-33-5
Library of Congress Control Number: 2022933043

This book is published with the support of the Literature Translation
Institute of Korea (LTI Korea).

FIRST EDITION

Printed in Canada

CONTENTS

ANY DAY'S CITY

WHEN SOMEONE CALLED SOMEONE, I LOOKED BACK

TRANSLATOR'S NOTE:

This collection offers a selection of poems from Sin Yong-Mok's earlier collections, intended to serve as an illustration of his evolution as a poet, and then provides a complete translation of the poems from his fourth collection, *When Someone Called Someone, I Looked Back*. Since that was published in 2017, he has published two more collections, the most recent in 2021, but the 2017 collection can be considered to mark his arrival at maturity in the development of themes and techniques that were beginning to appear in earlier volumes.

His first collection, *I Have to Walk Through all that Wind*, was published in 2004, when the poet was barely thirty. Further collections followed in 2007 and 2012. Born in 1974, he had passed forty before publishing his 2017 collection and will soon be turning fifty. He can be considered to have fully deserved the six awards he has received. At the same time, it must be admitted that there is a widespread opinion that his poems are so "difficult" that they are a challenge to the average reader, and even to older poets. In this, he is by no means alone among the poets of his generation.

The translator of difficult poems faces a difficult challenge since the translations should be as difficult as the original poems, but neither more nor less. One important question about any poet's work is what they mainly write about, the frequently recurring themes and topics. The other is how they write about everything. The first line of the first poem in this book is "At times a room is a tomb, so someone enters it and kills time making a mummy." Death is a familiar theme for many poets, and certainly for Sin Yong-Mok. One of the most significant poems in the 2017 collection is "Community," which begins:

> May I use the dead person's name? Since he's dead,
> may I take his name? Since I gained one more name today
> the number of my names keeps increasing.
> Soon I'll have all death's register.

The poem goes on to evoke responses to people and things seen in a cemetery, since "death seems to have planted eyes in me." But even more poignant is the poem "Lazy Corpse," in which the poet talks very openly of the mystery of death, leading up to his experiences of the death of his father.

> but only inscrutable incidents can be pointed at with a clear finger—
> cracks in a glass and traces of spilled water
> or the growth rings of a felled tree
> or torn-up scraps of a letter
> the color of burned ash
> the oasis of red blood emerging from the hot asphalt
> > of an intersection

> when the motorbike sharply cuts a corner
> and violently strikes the speeding taxi like a cross.

The corpse once concealed within the living body made acutely visible. The poem continues, struggling with the impossibility of coming to terms with death, whether sudden in an accident or slow as the result of disease.

Critics have focused on the related theme of sorrow, seeing it as one of the most clearly dominant themes for Sin Yong-Mok. Certainly, sorrow is a powerful factor in a number of poems, such as the poem "Flashlight" with the line (italicized) "There are rainy nights because our sorrow is still young," followed by the affirmation " No rain can ever wash away sorrow." Similarly, in the poem "Autumn and Sorrow and Birds" we find the lines, "since the word 'autumn' and the word 'sorrow' feel like the same word, / birds fall rustling like autumn leaves." Later in the same poem, we read, "crimson paint splashes over sorrow / and the painter leans his brush against a thought, of branches, / and stares for a time," and this points toward the culminating discovery: "So that's why bats are black! / Because sorrow and the body can be one and the same." Certainly, an awareness of fragility and impending mortality dominates many poems, such as the start of the poem "A Lie Just Half Told,"

> Nowadays I'm never surprised.
> Not even when a bird mistakenly tears its way into the sky's
>   blue flesh.
> It's just the trees' fault, like long ago

when I used to borrow a hand from sorrow, the master of my youth,
to toss stones into a pond, the trees
tossing all the birds in the park
were the water's graves that slept while standing up.

Yet there are times when the evocation of sorrow suggests that the poems, although they emerge from an all-pervading sense of sorrow, are in fact at the same time the fruit of a struggle to overcome that sorrow: "Through the sorrow of asking whether it's possible to think about life as / a blizzard's future, the water's forest, or morning that arrived alone / and the station of dreams." We are brought back here to what might be called the "surreal" aspect of Sin Yong-Mok's imagination, the way he proposes in a completely deadpan voice notions and connections that we have never come across before and in such a way that we cannot simply reject them as preposterous, incomprehensible, or unthinkable. More importantly, the mentions of death and sorrow do not necessarily sound gloomy. Death, one might say, is so much a part of life that it is at the same time unthinkable, challenging, and utterly inevitable, a touchstone for our sense of what is truly real in life. Lines such as the following are paradoxically comforting and encouraging, not depressing:

Thanks to the sorrow
your destiny overtook and reclaimed
because the dreams, snatched away, were driven out of your body
I'll live this death called daily life
until I die.

Generally speaking, the poems often start with a response to an everyday experience of life, then pursue associations of feeling in a very free-wheeling manner. In the earlier poems, there are some completely surrealistic topics indicated by titles such as "Certified Copy of Reeds," "The Wind's Millionth Set of Molars," or "Ice's Footnote," while other titles refer to utterly familiar daily realities: "Inside the Glass Door of the Seongnae-dong Clothing Repairs" or "Autumn Rain." The poems in the earlier collections are often arranged in fairly even-length lines, while a major characteristic of the more recent collections is fragmentation of sentence structures indicated by multiple line breaks at irregular intervals. Most of the poems are quite long, some even covering several pages, although occasionally there is a very short poem.

Instead of trying to identify a dominant emotion, such as "sorrow," it might be better to note a certain affirmative tone that overrides our awareness of a seemingly incoherent flow of images. The lack of logical connections, such as are found in a standard narrative, is the dominant feature of Sin's poetry, and the best term for this might be "defamiliarization." He provides constant glimpses into the free associations performed by his particularly fertile imagination, inviting the readers to accompany him without having any idea of where they are being taken. Once we learn to let go of our need to think we understand everything rationally, we can savor to the full lines such as these: "In the alleys the whirls of the stars' fingerprints turn in the locking direction;" "I'm living as the man next door;" "I am hidden as a feeling of rain." Far indeed from what is familiar, and therefore welcome, because we do not need a poet to tell us things we already know, or talk about life in terms that we already use.

At this point, we can ask the poet to formulate a way in which he might want to express all this: "Poetry has taught me that my body is a place into which everything sinks and a place where everything is connected! Small things and larger things, past and present, even life and death . . .To show that these things exist substantially while writing poetry I came up with the idea that my body might exist! The sorrow that comes visiting my body is proof that all these things are using my body!"

Sin Yong-Mok is an intensely intuitive poet of the inwardness that gives rise to all true poetry. The external world as such is meaningless and remote. It is only when it becomes part of the poet's inner self that poetry can arise and the poet can be sure of existing as a poet and as a person. For him, sorrow is not regret at loss, an elegiac mode, but the awareness that all that exists is present within him, at the same time as being and as non-being, all equally alive and progressing ineluctably toward death and oblivion in its very mode of being, an essentially tragic mode, and therefore sublime.

More significant still, the phrase "everything is connected" offers a vital clue to how the poet sees his work. His poems, he suggests, embody all the experiences first embodied in his physical body with its memories, emotions, and expectations. Like everyone, the past is buried deep within him, while the present passes constantly, a ceaseless flow of images, thoughts, and feelings, which are informed and transformed by randomly occurring memories from the past, which rise in great confusion by mere association, often unconscious. The future is equally present as the great white screen onto which dreams, hopes, and fears are projected by the reflective imagination. Each poem stands as an image in words of a moment in life's unceasing flow, showing concrete examples of interconnected images rising into the poet's writing consciousness. No need, then, to be puzzled or surprised if the flow seems incoherent in terms of standard narrative models. The embodied mind has a logic that rationality knows nothing of, while the human heart ever rides a roller-coaster of emerging images and emotions over which it has no control.

It might be that for the poet, the poems he writes and publishes for us to contemplate are an extension of or an alternative to the act of intimacy he occasionally offers in baring a shoulder to reveal the tattooed tiger lurking hidden there:

> There's a tiger on my left shoulder that's climbing a hill at daybreak.
> And now
>
> it's Tuesday when fallen leaves die coldly on winter's ground.
>
> A blanket that I covered myself with spreading endlessly in a dream
> snow falling and
>
> when the water in the kettle on the stove boils with the sound of artichokes
> this phrase comes to mind.
> Death is the experience of the gravitational pull of a world we cannot know.
> I write the phrase down and ponder. What might it mean?
>
> Snow falls.

In a few sparse words and lines, we have moved far from an Australian-made tattoo, far deeper beneath the poet's skin and muscles, to discover the secret tiger of the dreams and fears hiding there. If the poet's shyly bared tattooed skin is lovely, how much more so the confessions of the abrupt transitions of memory and association that compose his inner life.

In the end, the secret key to Sin Yong-Mok's poetic imagination might be hidden in his shortest poem, so short that it says everything:

"A white butterfly is not like anything in this world. Any child pursuing it is sure to fall down."

The beauty of Sin Yong-Mok's poems is like that butterfly and we are the children falling down as we pursue what we wrongly call their "meaning" instead of letting them flutter freely ahead of us through the familiar world and the world of dreams, suggesting patterns of association that owe nothing to the constraints of prosaic reasoning. Then we discover that their dominant characteristic is not gloom or sorrow, but a smile as bright and mischievous as that frequently seen on the poet's own face.

A number of the earlier poems in this book were translated with the help of Chung Eun-Gwi, Professor at Hankook University of Foreign Studies in Seoul, and the most recent collection owes much to the help of Yu Chang-gon. The general edtior of this series, Jake Levine, undertook a thorough stylistic revision of the text and proposed numerous improvements and corrections. The result is a far more accurate and poetic text, for which the original translator is deeply greatful. We'd like to thank LTI Korea for their generous support for the translation and publication of this book. Additionally, we'd like to thank the journals Asymptote, Wasafiri, and Puerto del Sol, where many poems from this book originally appeared.

A LONG-CLOSED WINDOW

At times a room is a tomb
so someone enters it and kills time making a mummy.

A room lying alone after erecting alleys.
The morning sun has pasted a window-sized poster
on the opposite wall.
Crossing the bright square pattern

is the sun trying to guide the world? The sound of children running
laughter, the distant sound of playing, but

it was only as I passed through her that I became an adult.
Arrested for the fingerprints left on her body
I have to become a parent again in a place of eternal exile.

Even though occasional gusts of wind passed
after knocking at the door
I couldn't get up
until the sunlight slid across the floor
and slipped out the window again.
Like how memories always open toward uncrossable places

any excavation happens belatedly.
Inside a black world where a white daytime moon
crosses toward oblivion carrying all the tombs on its back

there's no knowing when the mummy I made might be found.

Beyond the window, autumn mountains are burning.
I want to hang an iron cauldron between the valleys.
The rice that fills the wind's cauldron-like snowflakes
my sleep will gulp it down.

AN ISLAMIC MOSQUE

Every afternoon light, briefly, lies down here. As if treading along the end of a cave, I had to enclose the last stage opened by a road wrongly taken inside a retina shattering whitely. Inside this strange time, there's a desert, a river flows, and if you follow the remains of flooding through a long, long sandstorm, there lives a tribe that hopes to go into outer space, a tribe whose eyes have grown white after counting the stars day and night with their sixty fingers. Inside black souls robed in red leather, I saw Saracens' sorrow. As the echo of Salah slid over the marble, I read my name among the incomprehensibly printed letters and it staggered me. These people who were unable to go into outer space, because the land built by God had betrayed God's buoyancy, they had fifty fingers cut off, and with their remaining ten fingers, they erected columns. With these long prostrations, the flooding would not have risen beyond the river's water level, so the mosque might have buried numerous fingers. Still with white eyes, on the road wrongly taken is hidden a longing to spread ribs and touch. Just as the sound of a bell coils around the emaciated tribe and extends outer space, I spread my ten fingers in front of the unfamiliar letters. Due to the columns, resembling light's body, the ground's air became lighter and outer space was so far away.

INSIDE THE GLASS DOOR OF THE
SEONGNAE-DONG CLOTHING REPAIRS

In an alley bent like a carp's backbone
sunlight too is bent. Time, a hunchback too
has a hard time traveling
so between galvanized iron walls sits
a sewing shop with a low glass door.
At nightfall when earth's tilt coils the sunlight
sometimes girls
might look at the shop from a distance but
what they see is just their white faces
reflected off the dark behind the glass
and whoever it was that walked up that alley
that turned into a sheet of paper
must have wondered what lay inside the glass door.
Sometimes to turn up the legs of newly-bought trousers
a customer pulls at the door handle
like it's a cover of a fairy tale book.
But the old wife's not there
just the husband spitting out a bit of thread
who, with amphibian eyes, greets you briefly.
If someone shows him
the length of the trousers with their thumb and forefinger
he pretends not to understand
just vibrates his gills then soon
as if to train someone's needle's eye in biting

he begins a backstitch that looks like an ellipsis.
Inside the glass door is a wave
that no one coming out expects
as the husband checks the rake
of the thin, ever-thinning needles
in the two fins lying on the sewing machine.
Threads with buoyancy float about
and a carp that lives on thread hides there.
Sometimes a newspaper comes flying and knocks at the door
but the door doesn't open. If it frequently allows time to enter
the carp's scales will grow dry, so the glass
obstinately keeps its dentures clamped shut.
Next to the bent alley, there's a sewing shop.
Since all the Seongnae-dong people
have gotten thin like paper
no one has taken a peep inside the glass door.
Like how a fluorescent tube gets bent in a fish tank
whenever people pass the store
they can't avoid their footsteps from twisting.

THE APARTMENT DWELLER

In a thousand years' time, this will be a sacred shrine.
The apartment.
On a board in front of the janitor's lodge
my descendants may see a notice:
    To be allowed to lie down in these magnificent ruins
    one must endure hard labor
    and painful contempt—
Down there is the management office where I went
carrying the maintenance fee and my remains
which will later be pictured in the apartment guidebook.
One morning, sitting on the toilet
I thought of the apartment residents
who must also be doing their business, dangling their hands
a few meters up, down, apart
hanging like photos
of kings just after they took the throne.
Yes, the Roman catacombs
where the faithful sleep layer upon layer
and the sun powder
sprinkled like the blessings of persecution
the cloven foot of a camel setting off across a stony desert
a woman's face like a dry tongue
children chewing sand grains, the catacombs
where all these people live with their share of destruction
each body in each room where night comes.

Between one cloud and another, a banquet is being served
and sheets of time that transform earnestness into holiness
hang beautifully in every window.
If the era ends like this
I will be a martyr.

A FLOWERPOT

One day a flowerpot was delivered.

I've
come into some land. Soft
soil, I
will be buried there.

Passing in front of a flower shop behind the window
caskets are entrancingly disposed.
Trees and flowers grow lovely like burial mounds.

Sunlight and wind seep into 70 square meters of solitude.
Orchids blossom
and hunch-backed time enjoys a kind of honeymoon.

My grave is fragrant.
Though not like a butterfly
performing the dances of some distant land
one day I will set my soul afloat in that clear height
the void where flowers fell.

If I hug the roundness and wait, maybe I can grow old painlessly.
If disgrace is pruned away like a flower stalk
harsh longing might be able to die a natural death. Maybe.

One day
a drunken foot broke the flowerpot in passing.

A BUTTERFLY GOES TO A BUTTERFLY

The cobweb is the butterfly's body. It's the flap of wings drawn in the void by a butterfly that passed through the spider's stomach, the void a butterfly gifted to the spider, a rice bowl handed back after eating. The wind nods and permits the void's fluttering earthquake made as a butterfly calls a butterfly. By its blazing impact, sunlight says that if you dig down into the bottom of hunger, then longing emerges like a stone. Between spider and cobweb, there stands the butterfly's life. Something passing through the spider's body, standing as a cobweb, that's the story of my mother who hates my older brother for resembling my father. That's the reason why each time love comes to me, it arrives with a changed face. A butterfly goes to a butterfly and shakes the world. Shaken, it attains cold-heartedness.

A DANGEROUS BIBLIOGRAPHY

I'm feeding a cow grass and waiting for it to turn to horn.

The clouds' march lasted a long time.
The houses had front doors like socks
that were like the weather that yesterday stripped off

and left behind. While I was living in that house
the only thing I knew was a secret
and the only thing I didn't know was a rumor – and therefore
silence!

After putting on the mask I took from the mirror
I waited for the mirror to become my skin.

Wearing a scissors-brand mask, every day the calendar
was marched into yesterday.
The scissors gave me grounds for suspicion.
By cutting masks out of the shadows

the calendar pages flipped in the mirror.

That house was filthy. So many footsteps.
The cloud's left and right foot
and the partially clipped-out eyes and noses—but, nevertheless
silence!

Whenever the house was opened
the front door turned inside out.

and the white cow reflected
as a black cow in the mirror.
Just as the weather comes wearing the cloud's socks

I feed the cow grass and wait for flowers to blossom on its horn.

CERTIFIED COPY OF REEDS

Beyond the man making salt
in the place where crumbling shadows cross
are old attendants being handled by the wind.
Fields where salt rose once piled like snowy peaked hills.

Reeds darkening, robed in shabbiness.

One autumn as I walked along empty field-ridges
I saw flocks of birds that the fields were spitting out like pain.
They were embedded in the far-off void like so many broken points.

That day I wanted to hang an arrow into that curved body.
A day when every conspiracy supported a one-leafed sunset.

If the wind has strata too
the only fossil it will leave
will be the night.

My resolution was not the swinging of time's pendulum.
Like a scar drawn by a daytime crescent moon
the head of a family bent over
weeping with the wind's voice.

There is wind inside Father's bones.
I have to walk the whole of that wind.

The Wind's Millionth Set of Molars
(2007)

THE BIRDS' PERU

Birds' nests don't have roofs.
The solitude as they bury their beaks under wings
to withstands storms, and the stillness
of soaked feathers drying
must nurture the birds' wings, until, one day

a moment arrives carrying fate on its back.
At the heart of the city
the wind's upper and lower jaws
are clamped unremittingly
on a black plastic bag. The bag
suddenly soars up
impressed with bite marks.

The air's black target, its center open everywhere.

The whirlwind circles the nest
and the birds' solitude ripens like a horn.

Aiming to strike just one blow into the sky
the birds circle in search of a weak spot.

Reveal the bright air's dark windpipe!
If only I can attack that spot behind the wind's back teeth

like a truncated horn
I'll be able to devote my whole life to moving onward.
Oh, Death
set fate free!

Creatures sleeping with their backs to the sky, the tomb
of solitude is the sky.
Just as the black bag suddenly digs its own grave in the sky
in order to reach that exact spot

birds never tile their roofs.

AUTUMN RAIN

Evening clouds wash their feet
in mud.

Rain.

Gingko leaves bloom
on the ground like foam.

If every passing footprint is a sentence
are many tales erased here?

Or do they get completed?

In this time when birds, fitted with the wind's bones
spread their wings
in birdcages made of flame

the darkness shining out of silence is a sculpture, is a bust.

Cast off your legs and
advance through the night
without leaving footprints.

A faint dream borrows birds' wings and links tales together.

A sentence made
with the mud lump's body rolling over the ground
whip unfurled

slapping that face.

A CLOUD'S FUNERAL

In Gurye's deep valley
I stood at the ferry landing with no light.
The water's surface ulcerated by falling rain.

I longed to hang a funeral banner
from a green-leaved bamboo
and plant it somewhere in that flowing stream.

If I scoop up a handful of your green light that vanishes incredibly
if the clouds are white, the white cloud will float northward.*

Even standing with my body soaked
when water flowed
pebbles kept rolling inside my body
as if I was a river bed.

As the water that mounted the rocks and fell dreamed moss dreams
the water drenched with the blood of pines dreamed pine-needle
dreams.

My feet sunk into the dark blue sky as if taking a dead man's pulse.
Funeral bier sounds, bier sounds aching.

If the riverbank is a coffin, then the estuary digs graves.

Wandering the empty ferry landing
soaked with you, no kind of earth
will ever welcome me.
Could it be that the wind is a public cemetery?
When I set my foot into the sky

holding a black umbrella, I become a guest of yearning.
I am a child mourner who borrowed the chief mourner's headband.

* From the poem by Yi Yong-Ak "Child, Let's cross the Stone Bridge"

PUTTING NOODLES INTO BROTH WITH A RED FACE

Water's shoes that water wears to walk in.
Water's footprints printed on the water.
Water borne on water's back and water embraced by water.
The red wrapper, that's water's bottom
and beneath the wrapper, that's water's exterior.

I put noodles into broth.

In the bowl from which hunger, robed in a body of white steam, rises
the noodles are rainwater's gray hair.
What labor is that dangling from every chopstick?

The Gungdong bus terminal.
Foreign workers with red faces
wait for the far side of the Earth.

Rain falls.
In life's prison
fingernails made of air are being scraped by yearning!
The rain gathers.

The Gungdong bus terminal.
Foreign workers with red faces
are eating up this side of the Earth.

In the bowl where memories are twisted and lifted as white noodles
streaks of rain, the heart's white hair.
What name is that raised on every chopstick?

I put noodles into broth.

The afterimages of faces rising on faces
and the shadows of faces remaining on faces.
Faces fixed on faces, and faces
overlapping faces in the heart, the face's floors
and, in memories, the faces' exteriors.

CHEERFUL ROUTE

Cheerful Bak Gu-Cheol went to heaven. On the road to heaven
birds drew creases every day, erasing his footprints.
It was impossible to follow him.
And yet, eager to climb up to heaven too, the birds leaped down.
From roofs, from windows, on bridges
they fell without end so that they could rise again.
They abandoned their bodies.
But, without wings, how would they ever be able to reach heaven?
Gaining height briefly then losing it again
breaking magnificently through heaven's gravity
that they had to break free of, they are jet planes
soaring downward.
Cheerful Bak Gu-Cheol was sent heavenward. In their burial plots
the birds buried themselves. Intent on sending themselves heavenward
they blocked up noses, blocked up mouths, blocked up ears
imprisoned themselves in squares
covered themselves with earth trampled hard.
If they equipped themselves with buoyancy
they would never be able to reach heaven.
A coffin that turns into a shoot sprouting toward the distant heavens
is like a spaceship. A grave dreaming of the slowest and hardest flight
is the sturdiest launching pad.
In the world, there's a cheerful route.
Birds, too, fall to earth in order to go to heaven.
They seep into the earth, and slowly
arrives the spring.

RACK WORSHIP

In this village there is a tradition of execution worship.
A rack is fixed to the top of every lofty roof
and elaborate praises are launched into the air.

The wind tugs at the racks' red fluorescent tails.

Every morning when the cross's shadow fell
the sound of amputated footsteps rose
and perched on trousers as black stains.
On days when the sounds of shared prayers
covered the ground with damp patterns

I tiptoed up and down the stairs but
nothing but shadows occasionally dropped from the rooftops.
No matter how many nails were driven in
the night was never pierced.

A village where only the wind
winding round the racks hardens into crimson blood
in the westerly sky, like asking the reason why long ago
as if by some kind of execution, you

were excluded from this place.

I wanted to ask the reason
why I was abandoned here, laundry flapping
on the roofs of soon-to-be redeveloped row houses

laundry playing energetically
with white trouser legs
leaping in the wind.

I WANDERED AROUND WEARING WET CLOTHES

Whenever I awoke from sleep, my house was soaked with water.
In every dream I poured out my father.
It would be better if it broke, that water jar.
I knew it was full before I even looked into it.

I couldn't carry the jar on my head.
Father needed to be at home.
Wet clothes always clung to my back.

Trees grew up again and were rained on like laundry.
I wanted to squeeze the trees tightly in the jar, spread them
on the warmest place on the floor.
Whenever I woke up

the water jar was spilled and I longed to drink it.
Digested father, excreted father.
If I turn around, there's always the buzzing of wind in my ears.

Crying things are hollow inside
the sound that comes out of a pipe if you turn it.

My father appeared as if someone grabbed him
and was spinning him around.
Father, father, father

even if I dipped my head in the water jar and called for him
there was never an answer.

Why do all the tree leaves have the same color?
Why do all the boughs point in different directions?

As I woke from sleep, the houses were wearing wet clothes
headed somewhere in a line.

DAECHEON PORT

I looked at the horizon for too long. My eyeball got slashed.

On my way to my lodging, I was in tears.

But it was too late to cry.
High and low islands had their ankles wet to the same height.

Lights that have taken over a few sunsets
have woven the islands together and lit a fire, here
at Daechon port, where

countless horizons have been drawn.

On the sandy beach
in order for the waves sharpening their blades to forge railings
the beach calls forth a heartbreak
into the seagull's cries and the smell of clams cooking
that can't even be prevented by breakwater
are a heartbreak
that is like a water stain passing through buoys of time.

The horizon crossed over my upright body
in the corner of a street bar
while I fumbled with a cross gone astray.

If a few fishing lamps shine bright, heated by fire lamps

faces spring up together, equipped with gills.
Swimming through the red glow, divided into the dark backs of ark
clams

I wondered, why are there no waves in liquor glasses?
The sunset that you fish from your body
by using the bone of the sea as bait
spreads out as the rising tide

while blurred islands roll up their wet trousers

I wonder, why do the fishing boats that cross the far horizon
come back to port?

THE WIND'S MILLIONTH SET OF MOLARS

I've stayed put a thousand years
yet I never got a fox's nine tails or an imugi dragon's black wings.
After a thousand years, my tongue has become a stone. As a result

talking about a pagoda is harder than building a pagoda.

However, when the smelly fins of the fish swimming inside the stone
circle the dark tower and the fish's gills pulse like toothaches

as it passes hidden stars, the wind pours out old teeth
like clouds it wore for only a moment and then took off.
In the valley of the pagoda is a pond in the air.

The bamboo that grew, tooth marks of the wind.

The birds that settled, tooth marks of the wind.

As it stood put for a thousand years
when the brow of the cornerstone of the old Hall of the Dead
glimmered as if under water

I wanted to make the evening dark
with a single round bite of a wooden gong

but the monk had no voice left.
Because prayers are the only fish feed
sprinkled on the stone's fishing ground

fish out of water flap around with aching teeth.

The pagoda valley is born
when the air is struck and the lotus pond is dug
and I am caught between the wind's millionth set of molars.
I am bent with a thousand years' tail
and I am broken with a thousand years' wings.

SEDIMENTARY LAYERS OF WORDS

The words I spat out
soaked the floor. They weren't
sucked into anybody's ears. When something passed
they divided like dough and left ripples on the walls.
Nobody tried to carry my words in their bodies.
Everyone closed the door and disappeared
and no one came back. In the end, I
began to speak alone in a vacant room.
The words I spat out filled the room from the bottom up.
Soon they exceeded my height. From then on
I gave up walking. With a long soft tongue
I swam about in my dough of words. And all the while
I spat out words endlessly. The more I spat, the more completely
the words stiffened like stale dough.
Sometimes the wind blew through cracks in the door
the sun shone in
and the dough hardened. It grew more and more difficult
for me to move until finally
I couldn't move at all. As all the words
dried up completely, I fossilized
like a rumor. The last moment came
as I was wiggling my fingers. That accidental posture
became my eternal body.
In about ten thousand years, a geologist
may discover a species of tongue

hidden in the sedimentary layers of words.
I shall provide evidence of a ruined poet.

Any Day's City (2012)

EXPLODED SPRING

I did not explode. And as nothing has hit my temples
I have not exploded.

A balloon running away
with a tail hanging on its wind hole.

There's no battlefront in my direction
just an endlessly receding backline.

In any corner I look are the collapsed things that used to be bodies.
I look at things that once were gunpowder.

There's no direction in spring's battlefront
just an endlessly approaching hollow.

As nothing has hit the temples of spring
spring is running covered with balloons made of light.

Fat targets are smiling.

AN ALLEY WITH FALLING MAGNOLIA BLOSSOM

I came along an alley where a bread bag was blowing about.

Who had eaten the contents and thrown it away?
Someone with the contents inside them, so becoming the husk

the person had torn open the bag and eaten the bread.
My body, once it had turned into a bread bag
swept the alley to brighten it up.
(After tripping over a magnolia tree's empty trunk
my body was stabbed by the red graffiti
on a redevelopment fence and turned inside out)

Bloated, my body soared high into the sky and ripped somewhere.

A child kicked at it in passing. A rat ran away covered with it.

Someone ripped the spring here. White on the dusty ground.

Spring came pouring down, stamping
until someone devoured it completely.

After devouring it, that person became spring's husk.
Became a bag.

The wind was my bag. The wind, the void with its body ripped somewhere

came along an alley where a bread bag was blowing about.

A TANK TRUCK

Cloud: boiling ice.
I saw windows melting all day long.

The sleep of someone dying, burning brightly.
Poking with iron rods at quilts tangled like flames

the sunshine was stuck at an angle.
The curtain is fluttering.

It's the work of flocks of transparent birds with wings formed of ice.
In the broken, glittering air
when endlessly surging heat is burning in damp fires

when the ash of water burns white swirls in the depths of breath
it's the work of black beds flying out of windows.
Someone is freezing in their dreams

with the face of a tossing cloud.
With a body boiling coldly.

There was one explosion over there.
Like the flames of sunset drawn by every torn scrap of wind
when the darkness finally draws away every color.

I wear one layer of each shade of ash.

Body, playground of blood.
I believed that I was running ceaselessly.

THE MOMENT THE TIP OF THE TONGUE TOUCHES A KNIFE TIP

The moment the tip of the tongue touches a knife tip
water vanishes from the sink.
The water's gurgling sound follows tens of thousands of blood vessels
and penetrates the air's skin
like a knife with a broken handle, and
abruptly

the light that falls headlong from a fluorescent tube
is time's white soles trampling ribs.
The lights of the shopping center beyond the double sash
chew gum.

And we believe we are immersed in this place.
How hard it is to live without pouring out.
We slosh briefly, gurgling
with faces immersed in waste water.

The body destined to escape from the bottom of this vortex
is a bucketful of body.
When wrongly pooled in the light of living
a letter comes into the silence
carved like the scar of a blade on a chopping board.
Fallen leaves, are they

the result of suicide or assassination?
The scene of a shout that no one answers
like a robber
like a knife with a broken handle, abruptly
a falling red tongue.

Look, calm is poking the moment.

When water vanishes from the sink
when lights faraway and nearby
mingle and the mutilated moment
scatters its body in the air
I kill because
I love this place too much.

ICE'S FOOTNOTE

There are times when suddenly
a rectangular kite can be seen stuck in the distant sky.
When I slipped

and fell
I saw a fallen leaf stuck in the frozen lake.
I thought of a fish's mask, wearing it.
I wanted to ask after you. Where are you passing now?

No chance has been demolished here, now
where of all things, winter is.

When we look at each other with eyes of ice pierced round
either we're wearing water's mask
or water's wearing a mask, superimposed as one face.
Is that water's physiognomy or a physiognomy mirrored in water?

To become a perfect target, a lake locked up a ripple.
The sun's sunken eyes are
greetings to a chance growing old
and the future to a bad habit.

When the wind twists its body into a centrifugal force
suddenly, the rectangular kite stuck in the distant sky disappears.
Its face unstoppable though frozen hard.

To reach this place, you need to fall in the posture of a fish.

To get out of this place, you need to flip. With the eyes of a fish
I slip

and fall
and suddenly
there are times when you can see a harpoon stuck in the sky.

FIVE SECOND'S TECHNIQUE

Wheels are attached to his bed.

The world five seconds after running while lying flat.
The world five seconds before waking up
after touching reality somewhere in a dream

Wheels pass through chance.
The technique of proceeding, the technique of stopping, and
the technique of not returning.

Gateway of sleep! The mansion five seconds after
resembled an evening one hundred years before.
The front door five seconds before, a morning a hundred years after
a bed with wheels is passing through.

The technique of a hundred years opening and closing
like the padlock attached to the door of sleep

A wheel spins and one moment rolls.
The engagement of gearwheels turning in opposite directions
from the earthworms who've made earth their dining table
to the people whose grave is the earth.

The joke cracked by revolving things.
Dreams and reality intersect like the beds of an emergency ward

when getting to sleep
when waking up in a flash

the technique of murder practiced for five seconds.

Whether or not a body is finally
either the wind's future or the sand's past.
Whether the wind forms a whirlpool of twisting sand
or it becomes that mansion.

— finally, advance!

WATER'S PICTURE BOOK

Digging into the back of a prostrate animal, I planted a tree.
To stand and run
until blue eyes flare up as autumn foliage
until a red feather flaps as a fallen leaf

I am someone with a shadow hanging in tatters
washing the inside of a window frame
that heavy rain passed through.

Longing is always at the very top or the very bottom
so that if I turn the faucet on it's either gushing lightning or thunder.

Suddenly, the floor I drew as a circle
to give brighter eyes to vanishing things
deepens like darkness.

I dug into the animal's back and planted a tree
as a moving green forest, as a red throng with a leafy shade on its head.
And then the water nourished the tree so it could stand up
and the water nourished the animal so it could run.

The water's black screams came bursting out in a logging flower shop
where a sawtooth's rake bloomed—in a hunting park where gun beaks
sucked fresh milk
of trees with hearts or animals bearing leaves
like the sunset glow vomited by human beings.

As I inherited cloudy blood at the start
I exchanged my body for a puddle welling haphazardly.

Like eyes closing slowly on the ground
I wipe away every place the body's girth stripped off
with the stain of the shadow roughly engraved
and wait for a downpour inside a misty window

until children grafted onto rocks burst into tears altogether
until children growing with hanging tears smash the rocks.

When Someone Called Someone, I Looked Back (2017)

FLASHLIGHT

Is a circle born leftward?
Or is it born rightward?

Does the home of a leftward-born circle belong on the right?
Where does the right begin?

Is someone who draws a circle its parent?
How many circles have I drawn?

Am I a sinner to them?

I went walking leftward, so why do I arrive on the right?
Why keep drawing circles?
What's circular?

What's circular?

When the flashlight beam pursuing darkness shone on my face
I was caught in the only circle.

Rain falls only inside the circle.

We always undergo exploitation of the most precious thing we own.
You were alone, and I was poor, of course
and above all, because we were young

everything is destined to grow old.

But the darkness could never be caught.
Every time the flashlight shone out
it ostentatiously retreated outside the circle of light.

Rain falls only inside the circle

I had barely begun to scream.
There are rainy nights because our sorrow is still young.

From the next day on
the sun hung in the only sky
like a plate immersed in a slop pail.

From the next day on
I thought about circles I could smash and circles I could not smash
but the night we first met was still young.

No rain can ever wash away sorrow.

You were alone, and I was poor, of course

when the hand inserted into the circle lifted my chin
my face was already broken.

NIGHT

A dark man cuts off my head and carries it away wrapped in a cloth. The old cloth is pierced with holes.

Through the holes, I look down at the lights of a distant village.

One day a pair of lovers find the cloth dropped in the village and look up at the dark man through the holes.

They each take turns setting a foot on my head.

AUTUMN AND SORROW AND BIRDS
—All the faint signs

Once the wind revealed in passing the fact that sorrow was a bird
autumn came, all the birds died
because the truth is that being in the dirt is the same as flying.
The painter we call the Sun
laid down its bright brush
nudging empty branches
and ever since the word "autumn" and the word "sorrow"
feel like the same word
birds fall rustling like autumn leaves.
The truth . . . as I said
I wanted to offer another reason but
since it was autumn, when the wind reveals in passing
the fact that autumn leaves are birds
with things flying up and things falling down looking just the same
crimson paint splashes over sorrow
and the painter leans his brush against a thought of branches
and stares for a time.

After sitting for a while on the bridge, I suddenly realized
the only thing crossing the bridge were bats . . .
and the maple leaves' color is sucked into the sun.
As when fixing a ventilating fan to the sun
I am alert. While red light seeps from my body
and gets sucked into the sun, my body falls into the dark.

So that's why bats are black!
Because sorrow and the body can be one and the same.

Once the performance is over
once the lid on the paint can is shut and the sun has vanished
as I go plodding over the bridge alone, I wonder
if I can't go to sleep again today, what is it I should count?
Starting with one . . .
I reflect, staring at flocks of bats covering the sky
then I send a message:
Therearelotsofbirdshereasmanyasautumn

I WANTED TO SING A SONG FROM WHICH THE VOICE HAD VANISHED

I wanted to vanish like a voice.
Since the air, too, has its valleys
I wanted to go to a place nobody knew about
and when snow fell there, I wanted to vanish in whiteness.
Once snow drifts high, for some four days
the snowdrifts flow away like voices.
Since there is open space, wearing a fur hat, of course
I'll sweep enough room for at least one person to pass.
Once voices have piled up white, I'll sweep away just enough
so that someone coming from the opposite direction
can pass and smile.
Then, even if it's so cold it hurts
we can enjoy throwing voice-balls at one another.
If we roll voices into a voice-man
will he be warm or cold?
No matter, the voice-man will vanish anyway.
When I believe I'm walking among voices
the voices have already gone
and when I believe I'm making way
when I believe I'm smiling brightly
the broom sweeps up empty air
scattering it far and wide like fur falling helplessly from a fur hat.
When I believe there's someone rolling voices into a voice-man . . .
I'll end up flopping down, for sure

looking around like a snowman.
No crying, please! Your tears make time pass.
Make them branch into two streams.
Turn them into cheeks.
Days when your words were so cold that they hurt were good.
Spring comes,
like a voice I longed to vanish.
Every season's valley bears affectionate songs
and the songs, like voices burning white, eager to erase the singer
remain until about four days later. Of course
like snowflakes briefly fluttering through the air's empty valleys pass
from a silence to silence
like the way a snowman slowly drowns in its body
melting in the morning's empty space
I wanted to go flowing away to a place nobody knew.
But it's really far away.
Like the clouds of steam that billow up and come to a halt
above the great chimney of Dangin-ri power station
when I lift my head
like a song where the voice has vanished.

A SANDGLASS

I slept again the sleep I had slept.

It was a sleep pouring out white like sand.

It was a sandy field where
if I called anyone's name
it seemed they would appear. How could sleep move so much sand?

I saw people approaching from far away shaking off sand.
I saw names shattering into sand.
As they drew near

there was no telling who was who.

Someone's beach lay stretching endlessly.
I slept again the sleep I had slept.

Already dreamt of dreams, I was listening to the waves.
When did the waves wash away all my body's sand?

When someone called someone

I looked back.

Even though someone did not call someone
I looked back.

MORE DAYS
—Bitter Moon

All the world's loneliness is a mealtime.
A red motorbike is standing propped
in front of a diner.
At six-thirty a yellow bus lets children off.
At seven the warning signal sounds.
As I chew, I realize:
Wow! I have a mouth! I have a soft gullet. I have a warm stomach.
At seven, the barrier descends in front of the rail tracks
beyond which flutter things like three-colored ribbons carried by
children.

Like a remote alley on a rainy night, a fluorescent light floating in
laver soup reflecting my face.
Sorry, my heart's not back yet, so I can't go out.
As I eat, I think:
I have a mouth, my gullet's soft, my stomach's warm
as if recalling the hardest thing in life
like being sucked into the long fluttering of three-colored ribbons
beyond the barrier after waiting for seven to come.

Then nothing will happen
like looking up at a train passing just in front of me
missing all the faces in each brightly-lit window
the warning signal sounding, and
seven o'clock disappears from the children's street

red, yellow, blue
as if aimlessly comparing
three different colors
and as for my mouth and my gullet and my stomach,
I mutter: *My mouth and my gullet and my stomach* . . .
I'm sorry, I'm eating.

EVERYONE'S MAGIC

Such a view can be said to be a view
that makes an invisible view visible.
I emerged from Samseong station
and every windowpane that held a sun like an egg-tray
broke beneath the streetlight when the sun set.

Once they have filled up their own height
you could say that walking is just people who barely avoid falling.
I've also heard that the reason subways were made
is because people lost their wings.
Walking the alleys around Samseong station, exit 4
while passing beneath yellow streetlights
you could say I began to cry. As I shut my eyes
the subway passes, grinding cheeks against the walls
reflected in the windows. Like underground tunnels
if the night is an invisible back alley, the streetlights are endless
          windowpanes . . .

Since the light stays on after the fridge door is shut
you could say that you can see faces freezing brightly.
And this kind of magic, a magic that hasn't yet had its premiere
is what you could call a magic that repeats its performance.
As I pass Samseong station
watching a taxi appear in this building's windows vanish
and reappear in that building's windows

I feel that I might vanish or appear at any time.
Hurrying along like this
I feel I might be visible nowhere.
If I turn right I can cross the bridge . . . .

In the rearview mirror, someone hurrying closer.

In broken glass, even one person can create a crowd.
Humans have no end.

COMMUNITY

May I use the dead person's name? Since he's dead,
may I take his name? Since I gained one more name today
the number of my names keeps increasing.
Soon I'll have all death's register.

Might I be called Heaven and Hell?

Over there
where the man's name is being erased
from the lips of the woman being soaked in rain
prayers also have lost their way
and like the petals being washed away on the floor
now they are carried a few steps, stuck to your shoes . . .

I will reply to every falling petal.
Unable to find a welcome
after searching through the rain-soaked village
if at last sorrow, the collector of death
comes to me requesting a place to sleep
I will prepare a kettle of cold water
and one dry towel
and with that voice climbing up the body's creaking stairs
I will be able to ask, *What more do you need?*

But probably I will ask nothing,
fearing sorrow might want something
like a chorus of flowers resonating then stopping in a garden
in the vestibule's black umbrella
above shoulders . . . like raindrops
drip, drip

low eaves, window panes, stretched out hands

above them

as sorrow takes oblivion's pulse
then
says: *I miss him . . . I miss him . . .*
I'm afraid sorrow will cry
so I point to a far off, extinguished time and
like a lamp I hand over that person's name
in a register with nothing written in it.

I fear I'll be left alone. Floating like the sound of flushing water
in an empty room lent without the owner knowing.

The soul of water that is called a cloud
it brings the thunder and lightning growing inside my body into reality

in order to steal your name.

Come to think of it, death seems to have planted eyes in me.
The stone that took away your name is being rained on.
Ears have been added, like rain reading your name above a stone.
Blending heaven and hell, am I allowed to be soaked?
Over there, all the petals tapping on death
like the red lips of that woman leaving the garden
they are praying for me . . .
and here too

if life is possible
just as rain stops and rainbows emerge only when summoned
if love is possible
may I give my name to the dead?
May I call a person by my name once they're dead?

A LIE JUST HALF TOLD

Nowadays I'm never surprised.
Not even when a bird mistakenly tears its way into the sky's blue flesh.

It's just the trees' fault, like long ago
when I used to borrow a hand from sorrow, the master of my youth
to toss stones into a pond, the trees
tossing all the birds in the park
were the water's graves that slept while standing up.

Are the corpses of evening
autumn squeezing birdsong and painting all god's prophecies red?
Let's go back home.
Even on that day when the moonlight with the golden rim of the ring
that I last threw grew old with the face of youth pulling at my wrist
I went back home.
After cooking rice as warm as possible, cooking radish soup
setting the table, and erasing my mind
even if I sit down

and remove the heart of long tears from my eyes
and it falls like crumpled clothes
with a spoon clattering in the bowl
I walk on

wrapped in the spreading fluorescent lamplight

or if not, after returning home
after soaking my entire body in hot water
and wiping the white coat of steam from the mirror
I say your body hurts
and you say
like your body hurts
because comfort is something that no one can experience
for someone else.

I am muttering, indifferently sending
poor birds flying into birdsong from a place labelled 'I.'
If I just half believe a lie
the other half becomes true
or maybe god is like a gambler
fond of chance, spinning after mixing
a complimentary color with destiny.
And yet

even the bees in the park that buzzed through the summer
do not believe that fruits are living half the life of flowers.
Just as they don't believe
that flowers brought with them are half the fruit.
And yet, when we paid with our youth to have our fortunes told
in the whirlwind of stars
all the prophecies that we heard
were only half-spoken.

And so, the fact that we have become sick to fulfill the rest
is now not so surprising.

Even if every tree is God's arrow shot at the round target called Earth
even if we are holes pierced in the target
or are uprooted trees

since trees bury half themselves in the ground
I endure the night by thrusting a hand into a mirror
and strangling myself.

LIKE THE MAN OF CLAY I·GRADUALLY BECOME AS I EMERGE FROM A BALL OF CLAY

Because love is the time when a dream I'm dreaming wanders in search of me, morning always replaces a failed dream with a mushy body.

CONCEALED WORDS

God used up all the summer heat trying to sew the sound of rain inside rain. It was morning when, in order to retrieve one raindrop dropped by mistake, mists roamed the ground.

If there's a leaky roof, maybe water is an abraded stone.

I enabled that stone to hear the footsteps' sound.

One day at an estuary I picked up a raindrop, but no one made off with my footsteps' sound.

LAZY CORPSE

The target becomes accurately visible
when the arrow flies and strikes it
a beautiful whirlwind
but once the arrow has struck it, the target cannot rid itself of its name
and at that moment

when the blade slashes the wrist, it is like death appearing.

Here is the sea
vast, blue, peaceful
and until they're hooked
nobody realizes that creatures
with such sad expressions are swimming through it.
Fish, they are like the sea's arteries.

It might be hard to believe

but only inscrutable incidents can be pointed at with a clear finger—
cracks in a glass and traces of spilled water
or the growth rings of a felled tree
or torn-up scraps of a letter
the color of burned ash
the oasis of red blood emerging from the hot asphalt of an intersection
when the motorbike sharply cuts a corner
and violently strikes the speeding taxi like a cross.

The corpse once concealed within the living body made accurately
visible

so therefore, everything is already a corpse!

I had this realization on July 11, 2008.
I received a phone call from the university hospital
and while I was rushing there, Father had become a corpse.
Mother clutched the young doctor's grubby gown and shouted
How can a living body become a corpse?
Why can't a corpse become a living body?
My brother's tears were blood minus the red.
Setting my living body down beside Father's corpse
at the back of the hearse as it headed homeward
I messaged a friend:
Father's is the first dead body I have ever seen.

From that moment on I've only been able to speak
with the torn lips of a fish caught on a hook.

Rather, like the hole in a target struck by an arrow
to tell the truth
death is no incident. Perhaps it's alchemy.
I have never seen the beautiful cracks hidden in a glass
nor the mysterious growth-rings a tree has
until they were broken or felled.
But after all

if tears are mixed with red dye and injected into a dead body
the living body will circulate tears instead of blood.
No need to understand, of course.

Because the first time anything comes into this world

we reckon we have understood it already.

It's something like this. We understand music.
And if that's the case
aren't instruments weapons?
Isn't that thing that fires at the silence hidden in the air that rains
          down music a gun?
The singer that weeps before murdered silence
and you, too, aren't you a lethal weapon?
Slashing oblivion, producing sorrow.

That blade's true name is despair, a living body

circulating tears instead of blood.

I have no recollection of that girl I first saw
at my middle school entrance ceremony
March 2, 1987
amidst the spring flowers that winter fed its heart with
and the breezes that spring offered its lungs to
I stayed up all night writing a letter.

Some days later
I took the letter, returned unopened
tore it up and burned it in the most beautiful dusk that exists in my
memory.

I had failed to hit the target. So

that girl still remains a whirlwind to me.

No need to understand, of course.
Since there's no graveyard in my phrases for those I offered
like corpses that had lost their deaths
after that, I never wrote a single phrase for anyone else.

Speaking from the viewpoint of a fish with torn lips caught on a hook

here is life
vast, blue, peaceful.
In front of Seoul's City Hall and on Seoul Station Plaza
still burning Yongsan, shattering Gangjeong,
as in Moscow and Berlin and Melbourne too
my life was quiet.
I shot nothing, stabbed nothing, nothing,
things I could not break, or sever, crush or burn
like a lazy death.

I shall not return

to the house with a sofa with beige armrests
with windows that stars pecked at
where the front door opens easily only at night
therefore
off to the bar in the alley
in front of the house where I used to gaze at the rain-swept street
after ordering sake with raw mackerel, laughing
and chattering all night long and getting drunk

or as a fish unable to swim through tears

in a dimly-lit officetel
as a moralist loftily turning the pages of a translation
with fingers pure as a preservative
nothing but logic and analysis
into a religious life of truth convinced of being able to sort out a life
where blood and sweat and flesh are tangled together
into that corpseless epitaph

in a dimly-lit Izakaya
only capable of walking down a simple three-dimensional alley
after consulting a two-dimensional map, as a sociologist
into the combined chemical action producing the strangers' wounds
only treating itself, and feeling compassion for this world

time comes mixing red dye into the sea.

As a target struck by time's arrow
the moment the sun's beautiful whirlwind abruptly stops
and the eternity of a glass falls to the floor
or the tottering of a tree engulfs the teeth of a saw, or
the shriek of paper crumples and smoke's phrases are left as white ash

the void of the motorbike flies up over the taxi—
and from this spot indicated by the fingers of certain death

I'll never be able to return.

Letters caught on a faint fishing lamp
are transporting the sand of humiliation onto the shores of desire.
Into that unadulterated time—incapable of slaughtering anything
simply put
I'll not return.
But now, as the living body of a fish not yet dead but dying
I wonder, *When will the end come?*
The end is bound to come sometime, like a lazy corpse
looking at fully restored memories piled neatly as dust

things like Father coming home
one evening with a fish threaded on a reed
like the fish's gills opening and closing at the tip of the reed

.

.

.

once suppers over, for sure, Father's body is what I will have become.

SECRET FLIGHT

The altitude of a fly
flying inside a plane.

I'm on my way to Helsinki. Or maybe to Ankara
or an ancient city sunk beneath the Black Sea where rain is falling, but
supposing I arrive safely

I'll hang my wet socks up in a hotel with cups and spoons in pairs
one left unused
and quietly, as on days when candle light quenches the wind

from a restaurant where the streetlights raise embroidered curtains
will I be able to walk into the forgotten legends of a remote kingdom
that falls one Ramadan morning?
At every altitude, rain is falling, with no hint of movement
flies are buzzing
into serious talk about a wind-up clock
that strikes 180 times a day and jokes about death.

I feel as though moments vanishing like writing in fire
are looking up at me with bright faces.
Supposing I arrive safely, on arriving

quietly
like a candle lit in a corridor of a submerged city

will I be able to open a window?
Like a fly coming and going between one seat and another
arriving at an unfamiliar place, raindrops dangling from eaves.
Hoping to receive jewels held in secret by the night of blue tiles

can I hold out a hand?
Return to your seats and fasten your seat belts . . .
as I fasten my belt, the plane flies between clouds
and my blanket slides to the floor with a sound like rain.

PASSING OR NOT PASSING

This is the time when every shadow goes plodding eastward, then suddenly all fall and die at once. A lovely sight, no? While watching, I find myself wondering if the angels endlessly running out of our bodies are slaughtered under earthly light. I mean those endlessly appearing in my sight, my voice, the street's shop windows.

I've long been reflecting, when the gaze emerging from my eyes cuts off when I blink, then sees the shadows rolled up, convoluted by the wind then vanishing over the landscape, or by a nighttime window as they welcome my shadow returning home leading a herd of black cattle . . . what happens to my voice? Might a voice that shatters and scatters like a transparent leaf have an afterlife? Ah, if there's an echo, then my voice must also find salvation.

When shop windows suddenly light up

the mannequins really look as though they were once alive. Or else perhaps they are being endlessly slaughtered. After making love all night

morning comes, evening falls again. At that time on the streets when gradually darkening things suddenly become bright, I sometimes see born things being born and dead things dying. But it's not like I'm waiting. Because like streets that grow dark again all at once, there's no reason for granting rebirth only to angels born at the hour of lovemaking.

BEING DRUNK IS A DREAM

Somebody threw a stone.
Wasn't my head the bit of air that got broken off?
Isn't the hole pierced in the world my thoughts?
Since every kind of silence leaked out through that round hole

we're drunk.

Like light suspended from streetlights without falling

it's dreadful.
Thinking.
Like a knife blade bending near the heart
that a stone wound round with life's blood vessels
riskily left turned on . . .

I'm killing as much as is necessary.
Fortunately, today the drink is clear
so if I moisten the body's wick
like a spring wound up till it breaks
it will always be night.
Is night just the flash of a gigantic stone passing?
Might dreams be the forest where that stone falls?
Because anything can return where it came from
but not in the same way it arrived, therefore

thoughts do not heal.

Something we can't possess is wings
and what a bird can't possess is a wish to fly.
Because of its wings
a bird falls from the air
and because we want to fly
we fall endlessly from where we stand.
Someone never stops talking.

It's not because I say I want to fly that I can't fly.
It's not because I say I can't fly that I don't want to fly.

We came flying.

Like thoughts.
Like thoughts.

When one stone blazes
like a crimson heart at the tip of the knife that strikes it
emitting black smoke
like rain driving into the hole suspended above the throat
like sorrow

I'm dying as much as is necessary. Did you realize?
Holes break, too.

One body, not breaking, an everlasting ground . . .
One day

waking from sleep like a window breaking

taking my head in my hands
a pebble that came flying long ago gets caught and

tears go spreading like cracks.

LOVE

Just as raindrops vanish into the sound of rain
applause is heard when a candle goes out.

Everybody looks out a window at least once.
If only because of an umbrella they forgot to bring . . .

When one person asks, What happened?
There you see someone standing without an umbrella
while two or three people head to the window.

The third and the fourth person breathe on the window.
If again one person beats on a plate
everyone turns around to bring a glass of alcohol . . .
I'm looking for the person that wrote on the glass pane
I want to hold an umbrella for the falling rain.

If everyone says Not me
then who are we gathered here for?

Now there's no one outside the window.

SINCE IT'S US

I do not believe that someone's footprint is forever separate from their
body. I do not believe that there is weight without a body. But if you are
standing in each of those footprints, I'll never be able to leave you. So
it's not a matter of thinking some rain comes for some erased night. It's
not a matter of feeling that the downward drifting dark is scattering us
about like the shoes in front of a house where someone has died.

So it's not a matter of being drunk.

Ah, really.

Is it a feeling like something peeping into a secret room?
When the coffin was opened for the last time, laid out flat
Father looked just like a key.
While the stars make a single circuit, it seems
as though the world's firm horizon will open fully
when you bury someone.

I came back safely
I replied.
I went six stops in the opposite direction
after wrongly boarding the subway
but we are always speeding down the wrong road
always either increasing or shortening the distance of radio signals.
No matter where we get off

it's never a point of arrival. I turn back
believing I'm home safely.
We can really only get on with each other
in the hours when we do not remember one another, but
since the last person to remember each other
is also ourselves

when morning comes
the trees grazing the car windows take death as master just once
and it's almost time
to catch each dewdrop falling from eyes closed tight as night.

W E

No more star-gazing!
I hate sorrow being wasted on outer space.
On a planet where what keeps pouring out
gets emptied, on a planet littered with nothing but empty clouds

if there are crowds growing old slowly as they walk forward
following the sun

there are nights pricked with starlight
and even after despair has vanished like wind from this planet's blue ball
if there is something twisted, trundling along

might that be us?

Through the sorrow of asking whether it's possible to think about life as
a blizzard's future, the water's forest, or morning that arrived alone
and the station of dreams

since there is us

No more star gazing!
With those words, our despair was condemned
to walk the night sky, forever facing up.

Like the endlessly twisted moon
that goes trundling on
pricked with starlight.

A SENDOFF

What is being heated on this grill is like blazing maple leaves.
What is held in that dish is like newly fallen autumn leaves.
Amazingly, meat cooks to the color of smoke.
Or is it the color of ash?

My body is still full of maples unable to fall their leaves.

Yet they look as though they are burning red.
Every word is rising as smoke.
Every sentence is left as ash.
Every time I pick up a piece, confessions increase.
Regrets smell!

It seems that autumn leaves only fall because they slowly grow heavier.
It seems that stones only come flying when the wind blows.

Besides, it seems that fire is spreading through my body. Don't laugh.
I can see sparks in your mouth.

The autumn leaves have all fallen, so why is the wind blowing?

On that day where I asked that question, I'll never forget
how I gently licked an autumn leaf that came flowing from my lips.

It's time for fog-like-ointment for burns to flow over the embankment.

It's time for someone to squeeze out the river water.

If you look up at the trees, thinly sliced meat hangs from them
and beyond
dwarf stars can be seen, grunting as they die.

Is night really a black bag pursed at the ends?

There will come a day
when the leaves inside my body will all fall together.
There will be a sad ceremony that will emerge, tearing open my body.
Dressed in baggy pants, the season will stride away.

I will not use my body as the pocket
carelessly tucked into the waist of the season's pants.
I will not push sorrow etc. into that pocket
like a crushed cigarette pack.

FEARFUL SORROW

No snake can know what it feels like to sit down and rest
what it feels like to sleep lying down.

When I flop down onto the floor
when I collapse and roll about the floor
as though my limbs have vanished

is something no snake can know.

The reason why the frog's croaking
suddenly stops in a pond after a lotus leaf opens
revealing a night star

is the reason the light suddenly goes out in that house

like a snake passing by.

KAFKA'S LETTER

Like a lie, I say there is a time when you took away my night.

I have forgotten
the evening that was once contained in the bright store light.

I have forgotten
the dawn that was reflected in the darkened store window.

Like lies, gravestones once embedded in the moon fall and sink into
swirling alcohol.

All lies.

Then a white whale arrives pulling a transparent bone.
Like the first line of a letter being returned.

Life will not be something written down

Like records concerning an absent god intent on loving all impartially

life is being crumpled up.

SINCE I KNOW

Secretly taking the letters piled in a letterbox
of a long occupied house, suffering
herself instead of making the stories suffer
caught in those few lines of sorrow
that come flying from some unknown place
the girl walks on and on into the night's labyrinth.
I will teach this girl.
Since I know where to find the factory that refines sorrow by
simmering lives
the storerooms where the weeping produce is piled high
and the laughter turning on a conveyor belt
and because I know the mines where life is dug
and have seen the dreams that come walking out of those mines
covered in black dust wearing safety helmets
I know being is like a sandglass full of fine sand.
Once it runs through, there's only the floor
for the next day and the next, and the next
and since nobody flips it over
the next day as well.
I know that you broke my house's windowpane filled with black sand.
With your injured hand
you plan to buy green sneakers with laces tied around the ankles
and a pink star-shaped headset
but you will be all alone on the green street where pink stars rise like
letters in a mailbox that nobody has taken out, letters

which you have taken away.
I am aware of
the sorrows confined
in your nights
in your labyrinth
in your body.
They prevent the recipient from reading the stories
that the recipient will never read.
But you do not know
why you are hurting.
I will explain to you the past history of the sand
that bursts out when you tear open the envelopes
the origin of the letters that scatter when you blow on them
the night coming in green sneakers
and the labyrinth trapped in the songs of pink stars.
I became aware
when life was smashed into letters in a mineshaft of dreams
when your stories that were flipped over and over like a sandglass
filled up the cargo of a train
that you had read the letter that you wrote.
You surely do not know
you have stolen your destiny
from me.
I sleep the sleep of an abandoned mine, pulling
out the long darkness of a closed factory's chimney like a rod
and smashing the day. It's something you'll never know.
What gesture your little white hand made that day.

Thanks to the sorrow
your destiny overtook and reclaimed
because the dreams, snatched away, were driven out of your body
I'll live this death called daily life
until I die.

MAP OF A MURKY ROOM

I heard a voice that no longer called me.
At first, it was words, then a white-winged echo that had lost the crowd
like mist flowing down from the hands of dead stars.

The alley trying to rise somehow from the previous night's fever
is like medicine packets scattered over a meal table.

I had to eat in order to obstruct the replies
trying desperately to escape from inside me.
The morning of your voice
that left night screwed up in my earhole as it left.

Who was it that made humans to carry feelings around?
Intending to manage life between a dream and a dream
like carrying a smell from the supermarket
to the kitchen in a plastic bag
I don't know who slapped my cheek
then attached that hand to my wrist.

This feeling is leakproof.

In the alleys, the whirls of the stars' fingerprints
turn in the locking direction.
The plastic bag revolving from the wrist.
Now you never put your hand into the fog.

You never try to touch the damply cooling night.

Why do dreams have no ears?
No matter how loud you scream, you can't hear a shout in a dream
so why are whispers heard even outside the dream?
In the ally pills that stop questions are sold
however, this is a place where I won't use loneliness.

I heard a voice that no longer calls me.
So I replied.

Yes, I'm here.
Like fog flowing down from a star
while the sizzling croaker had to be turned over, I was watching.

THE MAN NEXT DOOR

Even in the middle of the desert
the cactus is immersed in water.

Just as a bird's bones are empty
though they fall to the ground.
Dead, a bird carries the sky down into the ground.
Darkness.
No end in sight and endless have the same meaning.
Night.

When I turn off the light, my hands grow endlessly.
They touch even death
then return and lie down beside me.

Each morning they take water to the desert-like grass sprouting thorns.

Mist spreads. In between
like bricks

I want to do some hitting.
Just like the man next door hitting the wall
while a child cries.
On
this
side

I am living.

Like striking a dead person's heart
bang, bang
hitting mist
weeping there
or

here, it's the same as saying he's living somewhere out of sight. Endless
or having no end

I'm living as the man next door.

HIKER'S REPORT

Somehow rain is falling with a hammering sound on a roof inclining
in the direction of hunger.
Unable to pierce the roof, the raindrops are sending their racket down
into the house instead.

An old house on a slope barely pressing on the shadows boiling up to
the ceiling.

A feeling of flames lies hidden inside that word "boiling."
Just as the roof boils on rainy days
swallowing the feeling of the sound of rain hidden in the flame under
the bottom of a saucepan
as noodle strands imply a feeling of the body flowing down like rain

my body is leaving pools inside the house instead of rain.

I am hidden by the feeling of rain.

The sound of rain banging on the roof
is desperately wiping away the raindrops striking the roof.
Lying on the floor, I desperately wipe away the sound of rain filling
the floor.
Since the raindrops' hour is further away than the hour of the sound
of rain

since the hour of the sound of rain is further away than my hour
I am merely boiling hunger.

Each day, time coming and going across that space
is erasing the hours of places that are further away.

From the shadows stretching away on the far side of the hours
to the hammering narrowly erasing ruin

rain is rising inside a saucepan.

LAKE PARK

Your thoughts that left your head are submerged here in the lake.
Like broken knives, they're swimming.
Like knives that have just passed through someone's body.

They're red.
Though they swim, they don't wash clean.

People outside the water, holding or placing their ears to the leftover
handles of knives
are saying something.
Before the leftover handles of knives
they are laughing.
No blood flows even if they slash.

You scoop out a carp's eye, eat it, then look at me wide-eyed.
Life sometimes consigns such moments to the past.
The feeling of being alive.

I said I dislike very much
the feeling of being alive.

Untying fins like smoke
the setting sun cannot be seen from a fathomless depth
therefore, if I swim upstream along the frontier called night
won't I reach the land of dreams?

That's why I'm asking.
If so many people fall asleep together
and if so many people dream together
how big must that nation be?

A land where only the leftover handles of knives remain.

There are knives
in the butcher's shop in front of the house I return to.

Thoughts that have gone past pigs are hanging there.
Because it was bright like the burning sunset
I cut off a lump and left it underwater.

COLD AND DARK

Winter uses the lake as a window.

So I threw a stone at the lake.

When you opened the window
it would've been good if I were there in front of it.
Thinking

in the afternoon cafe, there are doodles on the napkins.
The pencil is always knocked on the floor.
Like thoughts left behind, after sending cold, dark things flowing away

the sun is like the eraser fixed to the pencil's end.
If rubbed too quickly, it will tear the lake.

Let's not ask about depth like an idiot.

Wondering why the inside of thoughts is always cold and dark

I stroll around Lake Park after leaving the cafe.

Every year twenty corpses are pulled out. If that's true
the twenties that we have been killing in passing
must return every year.

Terrifying
when the time comes for the cafe signboard to light up.

Like a napkin that has wiped up water, fog rises
and since fog might not be the only thing in the fog
the thought of someone enduring something
clutching a sharpened pencil and

thump, the thought that someone will appear
who must have been there a long time, watching

as the stone hit the floor
then span and span on the surface of the lake

appearing step by step in the fog
like letters written one by one on a napkin
that someone seems to pierce my eye with.

If I think of a cold, dark place
a cold, dark place will surely appear.

As I go strolling around Lake Park
the fog seems to be inside water floating midair
or because it is like the moment a window is broken
because the fog is like lamplight that streams out of that window
even if the window doesn't break

even though I, sharpened like a pencil
will take another stroll around Lake Park
after sitting in a café sipping tea

whenever I write letters onto my thoughts
immediately they turn to graffiti.

LIKE A BODY THAT HAS USED UP ALL ITS TEARS

Like an expectation

that never once comes to us
though it carries all of us with it

rain comes, then

at a given moment, like traffic lights changing
as we shift someone's name around
step by step

like stopping after a long walk
rain drops and

sorry, it looks like I'll be late, so

first I'll send some snow.

A BIRCH TREE

Clouds tossing crumpled sheets of paper
on which questions are written
the letters pouring down as thunder and lightning
then winter came.

Snow fell, striking soaked sleeves in the air
scattering
like shards of chinaware that have forgotten life's secret
and in an instant
slashing a deep artery.

I was holding a stone.
The beauty of cracks broken like skulls.

Fragments that become one whole again
if put back together

but questions that never stop, I know.

When I met you, I invented too many flowers.
Spring, summer, autumn. Autumn
scooping up sticky sorrow pouring from broken arteries
to paint autumn's leaves
that one and only color.

As a fire was lit in the cold fireplace of a promise
winter came.
I was holding a stone.
At some time the stone went flying
toward the head of a gray-haired witch, but

like the sky broken soundlessly
bursting out or falling
questions

like responses not saved eternally
like white snow

we seem to share the sentences made by the soul.

Matching each other's secret letters

we saw
gray hair growing on a flying stone.

GRAY HAIR IS DESCENDING FROM HEAVEN!

Once past the black plaza, we walked on
taking our leave as if exchanging greetings.
Gray hair is descending from heaven!

We soon grew old
and the street was torn from a page full of red scribbles.
I just wanted to tell you about love
about springsummerautumn
but we had no nature left.
The sound
of winter and wind
flapping big ears while it flies away.
There, too, the faithful butlers called time will care only for us.
Gray hair is descending from heaven!
We rolled snow into snowballs uselessly.
We rolled ahead and got a head
and onto the torso that we rolled ahead
until it was finally standing
we neatly placed the head.
But we must not impose such things as yearning
on a snowman made of the cloud's mourning dress
water's corpse
and a unity of blood and tears.
We must not provide sorrow's witness stand.

A clown's makeup on the face.
Such fun! No matter how he's made
a snowman looks like everyone else.
That's why when we see a snowman vanishing
no matter how hard we press the snow
the thought comes that every time we cry
our tears are gradually erasing us.

Like a winter sky burial freezing white.

When the future flees from me

there are evenings that say the word *love* a lot
and mornings that say the word *hello*, but
I always believe
whatever comes up from behind me
in the world, when winter says *snowmen are real*
and spring says *they are all lies* . . .

DRESS

I saw winter demolishing the birds' nests.
It was quiet, so it didn't hurt. Being quiet
beautiful, ruin—it seemed to be forgotten
before I forgot.

Winter read an unfamiliar season from my hand, winter's Saturday.
I told it about one path on my hand, winter's best age.

The birds' weeping floated like bite marks.

When asked, doesn't it hurt?
I wanted to reply that what was gaping like a wound was time
a blizzard
winter's dress like firecrackers

the birds went flying upward. That's when I realized
the trees are winter's bride. Undressing
only in front of winter.

The wrecked ship known as vows, a black wound.

A tree stands leaving only a single footprint
but what fills up that footprint
and ends up disappearing —
a blizzard,
leaving only wings

like vanished birds.

Winter broke the stillness white
like bones inside the wind. It didn't hurt. Beautiful
because it was quiet, a love—even before it died
that seemed like it would die.

GOLDFISH OF SNOW AND THOUGHTS

Thoughts of you arose.
Like a goldfish floating with its white belly
upwards in the bowl
in the morning snow fell.
When I woke
it was so.
Thoughts of you floated up like the goldfish with its belly upwards
and snow also fell like the goldfish with its belly upwards.

Is that right? While I scooped out the goldfish
with blazing fins from the bowl
I thought if white snow is the goldfish's upturned belly
then surely the earth is a goldfish.
That must be wrong. If what floats upwards like a goldfish
were a lonely planet revolving around dark space . . .
would morning have come?

When snow fell, and the planet rose from the white horizon
if the thoughts rising had been you

then talk of the fishbowl would follow next.
Somewhere between home and the library
or Hongdae where I go to refresh myself
and Gwanghwamun, that I sometimes visit
even if there's a transparent curtain I cannot cross

I won't know it, and surely
nobody can smash it.
Like life turning around you in my thoughts
if I'm locked up I can live
or can be released after my death.

Talk of the earth follows next
and what is clear ·
is that white snow covers death.

Is that right?
While compressing white snow, I thought
covering its body with its body, surely
the reason that the goldfish had a white belly
was because it lacked a blanket that covered it to the top of its head.
That's right.
If thoughts of you were talk of a goldfish that never experienced snow
saying the goldfish had turned into snow . . . or talk of a frozen planet

then that's right. If that is upturned

here there's a fishbowl covered with a goldfish's white belly
and a galaxy covered with the earth's white snow.
Snow falls.
There is a night sky that your thoughts have covered with death.
When I wake up
I think

this might be the moment
the goldfish that swallowed the earth
goes swimming outside the galaxy, but . . .

it's a mild morning. Since morning has come, I get up and wash. After dressing and putting on my shoes, I open the door. Since morning has come, I walk over the crunchy snow. Taking a bus, I pass piles of snow, get off at Mangwu, and wait for a bus. I wait for a bus that had already gone by.

Snow begins to fall again.
Thinking something is wrong, as I let some snow settle on my palm
the snow melts in a flash.

INDIFFERENTLY

Beyond the window, there is a day draped in rain like night's beard.
There is a night with a hairdresser sitting on the roof
trimming that beard.

Like the way tears cling to pale cheeks like drooping ivy leaves
the window ultimately lets fall the rain.

So once the beard has gradually become so short that nothing remains
to be trimmed

autumn departs.

So once the white cheek has rubbed the pallid, tingling cheek all night
long

any time the roof encounters rain again
like the way tears cling to the pale night like drooping ivy leaves

there are days for looking at you indifferently. There are times for
touching the wet feet of the hairdresser who has fallen, his heart
stabbed.

MORE OR DIFFERENT

To a promise, waiting must be like warfare.
Walking along like sunshine
then getting soaked by rain in an unknown street . . .
To oblivion, meeting must be like a previous life.
Like a broken instrument, after gently flowing.

Hours being hurled.

Hours.
Hours.

I agreed to meet eleven o'clock at eleven o'clock.
I took a taxi.

Like meeting five o'clock at five o'clock.
I asked. "Is it beautiful?" The temperature of silence and
night's intervals.
In a place with beautiful music
everyone laughs gracefully as if they were meant to be.
It looks as though rain is tearing a windowpane.

Applause is like a botched musical score.

It was late
and I felt like going out for one more drink in front of the house.

Wouldn't that be beautiful?

Unable to put eleven o'clock into a taxi
we parted.

Flinging each other aside
we thought of one another. That was beautiful, but

I got no reply from eleven o'clock

about myself moving away in a taxi
and eleven o'clock moving away behind the taxi
and *Beep*, a horn striking time.
Sunshine rained on broken songs

about beauty.

In Teruteru, a restaurant in front of my house, a fish chopped up like
rain was lying on a chopping board. Was that music? Because as I
drank soju I thought it was sunlight.
There were people I met often and people I met for the first time, but
here nobody was laughing gracefully. Just then I heard someone say,
"Prick,". . .

Today again I took a taxi.

Eleven o'clock keeps its promise.
Every day I put eleven o'clock in front of me and drink.
"Your face always looks the same."

A WHITE BUTTERFLY

A white butterfly is not like anything in this world. Any child pursuing it is sure to fall down.

A BUTTERFLY
—Tattoo

There's a tiger on my left shoulder that's climbing a hill at daybreak.
And now

it's Tuesday when fallen leaves die coldly on winter's ground.

A blanket that I covered myself with spreading endlessly in a dream
snow falling and

when the water in the kettle on the stove
boils with the sound of artichokes
this phrase comes to mind.
Death is the experience of the gravitational pull of a world we cannot know.
I write the phrase down and ponder. *What might it mean?*

Snow falls.

Should I stretch out my legs and lie down somewhere?
Is it all right if I leave my face uncovered outside the blanket?

I was born in the year of the tiger.

Since death is stuck to a tiger's hide

snow always falls at the end of autumn.
Like ashes whitely covering the fallen leaves
that have not been burned.

Tuesday, New Year's Day, 1974.

Dawn toward the end of the eighth lunar month
has the strong spirit of water.
Nonetheless
It looks as though I'll not die on a Tuesday.
I wrote that line down too.
Why do I feel like this?
And yet

just like how all meaning comes on late
any reason can be traced if you look back.

The tiger climbing up a hill in an autumn dawn
is still there on my left shoulder
and there is water on the fire, but
it's all right
is what I erased as soon as I wrote it.

How old is autumn now?
Snow falls and

because there is a gravitational pull
drawing us into endless drowsiness
if we fall into a world we cannot know
then we'll be scattered at random in the air.

When we pile up by missing each other

as if casually putting the kettle down on the floor
I reflect
I'll put on a hide made of the ashes of water burned white.
At last at dawn with no dreams left
as I wake and touch wings broken as they were
and gently stick out my tongue

I flow clearly

like an arti, like a choke, the white milk of a butterfly licked
by the tongue of a dream boiling far away.

A SWITCH

This house has been collapsing for the past forty years.
For the past forty years.
The long shadows of migrant birds flying north tread on loose nails.

A leaky bathroom.

When the switch is flipped on, the sound of water stops.
Strange?

Talkative sister suddenly turns back to the television
and recites the following words
as if saying them aloud made them less strange.
The Men Women Parking Lot.
A pier lit by socioeconomic lamplight.
A birthday wound up on a spring.

Rain falls, it's night on the riverside and
weeping and the lovers breaking up
love entirely but part inevitably and
I've been falling asleep in this house for forty years, but

my corpse is still not ready.

Workers have come.

A damp stone emerges the moment they dig into the bathroom floor.
An inevitable ventilator turns and
a stone is found
in a drowned man's pocket.

Since early morning, sister has been practicing her script.
Driver speeding through my veins
because of your dirty boots my life is muddied.
And also
The leaver dwells briefly as pain in the body of the one left behind.

I put the stone in my pocket
and write in my household accounts
cost of repairs to the route of migrant birds flying north
then I flip off the switch.

RAIN STROLLING WITH A DOG

Instead of the first dog day
when a dog tied to a persimmon tree is barking
like a cicada
when I feel the emptiness of living these days
spent meeting you and being forgotten by you

clouds install sleepwalk above my head.

How about we go to the park?
In Jeongbal Park
where an old man wearing pajamas
back bumps against a tree in the morning
above a public air-walking machine
and hung on a telegraph pole
is a banner advertising new villas for an initial deposit of 25 million
and also my head

that the clouds use as a stepping-stone
because it's empty.

I'm sitting on a swing, the right one of a pair
when a kid comes racing up and stares at me hard.
Leaving behind an old woman who fans herself with a handkerchief
as if to say
being alive is really annoying,

I wonder, am I supposed to become a kind uncle
and get off the swing with a smile
and ask the kid, *do you want to give it a try?*

The cicadas are chirping
there's another swing to the left of this one, but

since this morning with a heart that's been swinging to and fro
between the decision to get off or not
like deciding whether to meet you
while the old woman folds her handkerchief
and wipes an empty mouth
as if something was there, but with no rice she spooned, no soup
she slurped, as if to say *I've consumed nothing,* vainly concealing
the dejection she ought to have felt from the start, and also

over there, to that dog being walked
the kid eagerly runs at the sight of it

as I inwardly tell myself
Bark dog! Bark dog!
biting my lower lip hard, I glare fiercely
then look around as if forgetting briefly
then again inwardly, I tell myself
I didn't say anything
as if to avoid feeling the dread at having to spend days in shame
from some words I would mutter and then never forget.

Plop!
I touch with my toe a cicada that falls to the ground.
Is it alive or dead?

Gradually rain begins to fall.
Am I no longer able to manage the tears I shed?

HOMECOMING SONG

I told a doctor, "The future is growing inside my liver." While I live
I have the feeling that the sickness occasionally visiting me
is making a home call to death in my body.

Father died of liver cancer.

A nephew texted "When are you coming?"
But more importantly
is there an ingredient called "Uncle" somewhere in my body? In my
body is there an ingredient called "Son," an ingredient called "Younger
Brother," an ingredient called "Lover?" Like detecting the taste of
sugar in spicy, red, boiling stew, is the doctor deciphering the sorrow
simmering somewhere in my body?

Is some ingredient in my body missing you?

Come to think of it, the blood that speeds around people's bodies all
life long, perhaps the reason people have children is in order to replace
this aging track with something new. If so, love is like constructing a
new sports ground for blood.

And if that's the case, sorrow is like the workmen hired for the
construction work.
Perhaps my life is sorrow packing me and carrying me away like sacks
of waste from the building site.

Father died of liver cancer, but when I'm drunk I feel that my soul is sloshing around inside me. My soul coagulates between my ribs, finally dissolves into alcohol, and goes flowing all around my body. Sometimes there are times when I pour out too much of my soul and it overflows. I grab hold of a telephone pole and feel like liquor glass adorned with limbs that's 175cm tall. Then I glance suspiciously at a plant or a dead leaf or a scrap of torn paper in a corner of an alley and feel like that thing is a stain made by some of my soul that I spilled. I wonder if scraps of my soul aren't still roaming around that alley like a bird that flew at someone and began to fall, fluttering to the cold ground.

Anyway, saying we got drunk together means we are sloshing at one another. Adorning ourselves with other faces then colliding, *clink* is to make a whirlpool in each other's bodies. Someone pouring alcohol into the glass called me, dissolving my soul in it, drinking it up, who is that person?

Who has been treating me like a liquor glass for so long? Sometimes flitting through the air in raptures, sometimes hitting the bottom hard, barbecuing pork belly in front of my life, who is that person?

A BLACK CAT

Heaven plays a game, putting a live cat inside the Pope's scarecrow, then setting it on fire.

Beautiful.
Running and spreading like a cat's shriek

night arrives to burn up every shadow.
In order to take away the black bags on the street
flipping black bags inside out, covering itself with a black bag

night
makes a black bag with the black bags caught and stuffed in a black bag.

How does Anxiety find the doors to knock on in the dark? Or is wherever Anxiety knocks a door? Like white snowflakes falling softly in the dark night, once the snow has piled high it forms a kind of floor, with *knock knock*, twice, or *knock, knock, knock*, three times, but like Anxiety, a single *knock* seems enough to boil the night . . . on a morning when all the people who know me suddenly seem to have forgotten me, like the cat I once was.

HOMO AMANS

I have seen the gods' footprints—left on the ground
proclaiming that they are human . . . (if they belong to the gods
they don't need to be stamped in just one place)
Footprints sleeping, waking, walking, falling footprints
and then at some moment
vanishing footprints.

To greet one footprint, the preceding footprint laughs.
To send off one footprint, the following footprint weeps.

Recalling one year's downpours, one year's snowstorms
and one year's gales, one year's earthquakes and tsunamis
like yesterday's twilight
a flock of sheep crossed over the season's mountains and vanished
leaving piles of stones on the abandoned ground, so

we've had proof of the gods' extinction for a long time.

They were dug either too deep
or too shallow, puddles
that collected blood during the rainy season, we called them bodies—
Stones came flying. Jumping like hearts, a deep valley
dug in a flash while the ground got wet, that's what life was called—
then every footprint hardened like a fossil.

While the rolling waves of blood overflow those depths
and complete this map's colony by writing the map

we have dragged along for far too long
the erased borders of the land called sorrow.
Therefore (like a procession walking forever toward a vanished land of
exile when following humans, the direction the gods went can be known
by traversing the evening like the stones that a flock of sheep has left.

Did the gods also trip into the puddles of their bodies and fall?
One year, because of unpredictable weather
pushing themselves up again from the ground and rising

I wasn't able to see the gods' handprints.

In the end if what was printed as the gods' footprints
is called life
love might be a wallet the gods dropped— taking out the few
banknotes in it
we bought big lollipops with swirling rainbow patterns
(our mistake is that we didn't put the wallet in the mailbox).

MARIONETTES

He gradually shifts the transparent bars supporting the clouds to a
eucalyptus forest.

Then he dips a hand in a stream and stirs it around.

With his fingers, he flicks fish off this way and that.

A storage area for water labeled "the sea." ·

The sky's balloon that bursts once every month
inflates like an invalid's breath
on a dawn windowpane.
After binding a puff of smoke to every chimney
he suspends the roofs aslant
the arcs are drawn by birds at nightfall

and set above a worker's head.

Each day he changes into the same clothes.
Even though they are entangled like children's hands
trembling in an afternoon classroom half-lit by sunlight
in order to not switch roles again
the father's clothes are there for the son.

One day
after sticking a blunt rice paddle into my head's small pot
and kneading the dough of sorrow in my body
and sparing some on a dish
he placed it on his meal table.
Beneath a bronze candlestick were red flowers withering
and clear liquor .
together with a few joking words fallen into a glass, but
I looked at a stone
that had come flying into the empty garden from a distant continent
and I said
Oh, I see you have a sleeping soul!
Even if you broke every replenishing reason
with the hammer that strikes with the whole body's pain
I see you have a soul that can't be woken up. I guess
you are living inside a dream that never ends.

He fixed the wings of a dead bat to the ankles of a child
who runs around the lawn carrying a yellow ball
screaming *Mommy! Mommy!*
Nobody could see the child's eyes
in the shade.

A DARKER COLOR

Finally convinced that darkness was simply a color, he set out in search
of a darker color.
A darker color, a darker color . . .

In his house, he had a sawdust stove. Every day he had to stir the hot
lump inside it.

Scattering on the winter's white snow pigments he bought from art
studios in the Hongdae area, *if I mix all the colors, night will come.*

But what he needed was a color that was even darker.

A color like the cold air his hands passed through when he scrubbed
them in a snowdrift after repairing the stove's chimney, a color like the
blackout briefly filling tightly shut eyes as he dabbed at a hand slashed
on the chimney. Snow is falling, cutting across the empty playground,
piling high even on the rusty horizontal bar.

Once back, throwing in more sawdust, *until the flame is burning
completely black . . .* he taps on the chimney.
Shaking the longest night with his own shadow, *but it seems I can't get
through the winter.*

Slowly the city wrapped in fog turns on multi-colored lights like a dirty
palette.

A fire that doesn't extinguish even after being covered all night long
a color like an eye that has passed through that fire.
A stream that doesn't run dry though it flows all night long
a color like a voice that has crossed that stream.

Even though sawdust is among the medical powders that can be
ingested to somehow thaw a body that's been frozen solid

if snow keeps falling like this, *what on earth can I use to stir up the night?*
How can we ever appease a darkness seething like *ppattjjuk?*
The stove slowly grows hotter . . .

He took a hot iron and seared his own shadow wavering on the wall.

Then adding still more sawdust, he muttered
Someone is throwing on white snow and burning up the town.
Finally, faint houses vomit out a darker night.

No matter how hot the winter is, the stove does not burn.

A DISTANT WIDOW FROM AN EMPTY LOT

The talent I most want to steal is that of piling up darkness, evening's
ancient art.

Suddenly light enters your window.
Even if one brick of darkness breaks coldly
night's architecture does not crumble.

Like someone hiding under black water
holding their breath for a long time

the talent I have is being embedded
in the exact size and spot of the window where darkness broke.
It's sorrow's ancient custom.

ABSENCE

Returning after a week
Sunday afternoon.
Opening the window, pushing the table aside, pushing the vacuum
cleaner around
I failed to hear the phone. Sorry.
It's all right. Sunday afternoon is the time for vacuuming, surely . . .
Where are you?
I'm simply vacuuming. As if a great swarm of bees had come in
through the window
the buzzing inside a beehive.
I'm simply moving around the house following a hole
that devours hairpins fallen from long, dark hair . . .
Let's meet next time.
Sunday afternoons are when people vanish.
In an empty house vacuum cleaners buzz around.
Swarms of bees that have come pouring through windows
push tables aside as they go.
Like bees that sting
leaving a piece of their guts behind with the stinger
while flying away
they vanish from the swarm. While waiting for a bus
walking along, holding some chicken
and sitting on a bench in Lake Park
people who vanish from people, leaving only their phone behind . . .
On being stung
swelling is like empty space expanding.

It means using a hole to fill a hole.
Like hairpins inserted into empty capillaries of pain
growing as long, dark hair
not bleeding.
Like the shape of motes of morning dust
that night has left behind
matted beneath the table, again one week later . . .
We cannot see.
Shutting the window, putting back the table, looking around
where's that hairpin gone? I'm sure it was there. For sure.
In Sunday afternoon's hole
a phone
is turning, buzzing like an inverted bee.

INSA-DONG

Like some long snake I've never seen before
water suddenly came spurting
briefly showing white scales, dragging its tail along
and vanishing into a hole.
As I grasp the tap
I'm like someone staring at a detached Buddha's head
in front of an Insa-dong antiques store
getting soaked in rain.
I grab the snake's throat and decide that
I must do the washing up.
Since the snake has so many colors
the water where it swims finally turns into dishwater
which is like how everything is with you.
A smell rises from the place where the water vanished
so I must open the window and do the laundry.
If I say this is about being erased would you believe it?
Squatting down and gazing at the tangled colors
swirling

the snake doesn't know it's getting dirty.
The snake doesn't put back on the skin it takes off.

At first the statue of Buddha
soaked himself in rain to wash his clothes.
Today the weather's fine.

Thinking about the clothes one cannot remove, cannot throw away
I want to write a letter that starts like this.

Even if it casts off its skin, the snake still has the same pattern
and while attempting to remove his clothes,
there's a statue of Buddha, its head cut off . . .

If I want to blankly stare at the roofs opposite my house
I must turn off the tap.

WHEN I'M STILL MYSELF

The water's boiling.
The water
is eager to disappear
eager to turn into
not-water.
Before it becomes
not-water
before it disappears

I drop in a barley-tea tea bag.
Snow is falling like leaves
falling from the spindle tree in the pot on the veranda.

There is me thinking.
One spring day long ago
people caught a bear, applied makeup to its skull
then released it into the forest.
When that bear returned all white, it seemed

it had been autumn until then.

Outside the window, the maple leaves that have not yet fallen
are welcoming the snow. One footprint briefly sustains
the ground of another footprint.

A thought that has not yet left is temporarily accepting me

to think of it.

The body grows warm like a shrine, like worship
sorrow gathers.

Since until then, it was just a thought

I was simply living.
I was still myself.

When I was boiling
it arrived.

Then it was time to cool down.

APPLE-APOLOGY

Autumn went to press the red button in the middle of midday's sky.

Like a very ancient teaching.

In a remote alley a boy and a girl slap each other's cheeks
to tune their loosened hearts.

The more they slap

I understand the time of flowers. I understand
that every color with genitals and the red scent

were turned on for a long time.

I did not know why summer and autumn, autumn and summer,
never used separate rooms.
Why night and day tumbled about
and tangled together into one body.

One evening stained with a remote scent
I had my cheek slapped for no reason.

The more I'm slapped

I ripen.

I couldn't tell why body and body, heart and heart
could not endure that hour.
Why you and I were obliged to be confined to that room.

Autumn went to press the red button in the middle of midday's sky.

Everything is falling downward.

AN ACT

You play the air
I am the wind.
Thoughts move concealed in the clouds
but maybe something will interrupt.

As props
the cloud is a bag with a jammed zipper.
A saw
a hammer
a half-cut piece of lumber nailed obliquely down, and there

someone passes by.
Overhead
half-done thoughts
my tools.

It looks as though it might pour.

I have a curtain's role.
I can dry invisible dread white and hang it in the air
simply by wobbling.

Falling, colliding, breaking
I can roll up and pin the pain
inside the rough wrinkles of the air like multiple dark-change wires.

If spread, screams
fall as the curtain's wrinkles

tearing up midday sunshine like scraps of rag
like props

I love you
from that confession that hangs as the rainbow of a moment
perhaps some corpse might pop up.
Thoughts
for a pouring role, clouds pull out and toss down stinging guts
and below

someone who passed and is passing
passes

soaked in rain.

A MOVIE IS LIKE A DAYTIME NAP THAT SLEEPS AT NIGHT

From the moment when the cinema was first built, in that place, only night endures. Like voices flying out of the body carrying away the heart's steam.
I was reading your name. You had died. Then, restored to life, you took a bow and said it was a beautiful night.

A child that had lost its way was crying. It was a night like unfolding a black umbrella. Rain was not yet falling.

But there is no night when you did not walk.

And there is no night when you will not walk.

Someone said that a certain love can never be managed by one side alone. Since I am still loving . . . He is not dead. I used to mutter, *such a beautiful night, such a beautiful night,* while I walked home when I used to live there. And it was obvious. A movie is like a daytime nap that sleeps at night.

THE WAITING ROOM

No matter when he arrives, I am someone who always says it's 3 o'clock.
I am someone who believes that three o'clock brings him. To come
down to this planet from far away . . .
It was always that way whenever someone shook me awake. In order to
arrive at three o'clock, I graduated and lost my job.

I lay weeping, embracing a shadow. The shadow has the body of
someone who jumped off a cliff. From a dream departing for the most
distant planet . . .
I wish someone would shake him. Then he would slowly stand up, open
the cliff like a car window, and gaze out.

How high a place does three o'clock go past? It must be a height where,
if someone falls, they smash into pieces without leaving a trace.

If a swarm of meteors appears and vanishes, then far off a swarm of
three o'clocks is seen then erased. Again a swarm of expectations
appears then does not disappear . . .
like a cliff stopping the fall of a swarm of shadows that never arrive.

When a dawn in the window in the waiting room grows bright, I believe
I am in a dozing dream.

I am running along a road barefoot. A red planet is rolling behind me.

OWNERS OF REASONS

It was yours. From the beginning it was yours. To give it back to you I walked, got drunk, and cried for a long time. It was yours, then one day a red ball came gently flying through the empty sky to my breast, and while it was flying the air split like smooth dough and showed the floor for a while. I might be welcoming the autumn of the person who rolled up a summer quilt and lay down in a park that everyone returns to. Or when, like a long, shining knife blade digging deep into my lungs, like glittering while wiping away blood in the lungs with rough breath, or when autumn perches on the apartment balustrade, stirring and stirring the evening, I did not confess to sorrow shaking and tearing its hair beneath the yellow lamp. That is not love, not honor, but since it's all yours, if someone embraces it like a stab-wound, then red blood comes rolling out like a ball. If I pick that ball up and throw it to you, the air will gently split again like smooth dough and show you the floor. I dislike that. Your memories recalling that evening glow as an execution ground. Like the dizzily trembling lamp of an interrogation room, your memories then hang that night's moon above your head. So I couldn't give them back. Even if one day I sit in front of the black table as if forgetting and gaze into your eyes as if I'm in a dream, still, there is the way autumn intends to end starting with us, and the reason why we keep borrowing small, deep shadows, and the reason why we keep saving them.

THANK YOU

I grip the edge of the table as I correct the "Thanks" I was about to say into a "Thank you so much." The table seems to have lost its arm. Time that nobody can embrace flows on.
It loses things through sharp edges.
What it loses are words. I spilled water, it did not run down. Straight like this, silence did not pour out. Finally, in front of the table being slowly covered with tightly clenched lips

how will the chair endure? Determined not to grab anyone, the chair will hide its arms to the bitter end. It's hiding its mouth. Like darkness that does not reveal its gaze though it stays standing outside the window all night long. . . . Then, the breeze erases all those words that have fallen under the spring trees, like a petal stuck to a window just with rain.

Has something happened up in the distant air?

Today seems like the kind of day when someone will rise suddenly and flip over the table. The chair's broken arms are shaking like branches. The floor is clambering up the windowpane to catch the spilled water.

As I correct the "Sorry" I was about to say into "I am so sorry," I lower my arms beneath the table.

A SNOWMAN

The future? Truly, if such a thing exists, I'll lose the wish to live.
Why? because I'll grow old, then die.

Salvation comes to me, not as I want
but as the heart I once wanted that is taken from me.

The darkness is so huge
in order to turn off the darkness

switches as countless as snowflakes are needed.

Among the people who are always alone in the word *together*
and the people who are always together carrying around the word *alone*
when I raised you

like the stone embedded in your eye

you cried.

WHITE MAGIC

After reading a novel about someone spending a lifetime in prison
I burned the book

hoping to release him!

Paper and flames and smoke parted as they met—
parting, they didn't even leave themselves behind.

Beginning with saying goodbye

mystery departs this world and
beginning with the body
the love
that hasn't gathered entirely from flowers and snakes and midnight

is the place where it locks itself up after it lets itself in.

SHADOW ISLAND

Once night falls
the shadow that I dragged about low down
during the day
wraps me in a large wrapping cloth
and carries me off.

My shadow will become a lover
I pushed off a cliff in some previous life.
One day, it will be flowing water losing her body.

So soft.

The flesh of darkness that can't be felt even if I swing my hand
icy

I see dreams through a hole made of sleep.

Even if they fall into water, day is day, night is night, so why are people
corpses? Falling into sleep, might dreams be the life of dead bodies?
Falling into dreams

it was mysterious that even in the dark everything still had color.
The things that you can still feel
even after touching them
the things that carry their names even after they die
were beautiful.

Might life be a corpse's dream? Like turning on a light
someone calls his name . . .

The depths of people are always the deepest when they are calling out
like, during the day, how the night pools.

Like a dream
his reply is audible . . .
Where? When waking from sleep
and staring around as if emerging from water
even like a voice unable to emerge from water
like listening to

falling rain.

It was mysterious how even raindrops had faces.
Beautiful, how there were beaches in voices.

THERE ARE NO STANDARDS IN THIS SORROW

At night. Even though I try to stack you up by neatly collecting, one by one, your footprints, your footprints imprinted on the floor are the landscape's magic that disappears as the footprints overlap. Even though downstairs a baby is crying as if it has seen something, it is like a footprint in a puddle or like a leaf that has redly settled in the puddle.

Outside the scattering sleep of a man that cannot live, a dream awaiting its turn

is, on the one hand, longing. And on the other hand, it is also forgetting.

KIND, GOOD PEOPLE

Even though only one person died
tonight death is born in fours on every white table.
The two pairs are quarreling.
In front of stew red like a dead child's weeping
Damn!
The two are sobbing,

Like a night growing dark because it's much too transparent

rain is falling, enough to fill the sea with an ocean.

What fate will death choose on its first birthday?
There is a thread for becoming a tailor.
Or a microphone for becoming a singer.
The two are laughing, making a row.
Crazy guy!
The two are drinking.

Because, even if you try your entire life
it is impossible to extinguish the candles
that fill a field where it is raining.
We don't have kids, and yet
because they are grown up
one day they'll come walking over. Because they were brought up
on the front of my arms

one day they'll speak. There will be a day where they will dream
a bad dream
and toss themselves into life, so should we fight it?
Always a new, first love begins
and one day, as they dip pork in shrimp sauce
they'll say "I miss you."

With the door locked
they'll cry for sure.
I'll spend a long time standing before the child's room.
Like people who say they're glad while weeping
like people who say they're sad while they laugh.

A DREAMER

When we hug we are all communists.

Out in the rain
pulling at one another like a taut washing line
hung like an evening glow.
Gradually emptying a glass of youth

the wind's

tale. Even on rainy days, there's a sunset glow somewhere. Since at every moment, there's a place where evening is approaching. Seeing the evening glow, there must be someone saying "I feel soaked in rain."

Then aging, I

will be freed from the washing line. With my arms crossed over my breast, standing in front of the clothes that time took off, I'll quietly quit.

Was that a dream?

Since I am just a body, like two legs, side by side, when I stand up
like arms finally falling in a second

I sometimes fold my arms.

When left arm and right arm intertwine, their hug makes me a prisoner
and then
I feel bound tight.

Being like economics

every moment solitude becomes the glow of the sunset
following the evening somewhere
like rain carrying away the partisans of youth

the breeze comes, the breeze goes.

FROM YELLOW TO RED

I stopped in front of thought and passed through sleep.

I ran in front of rain.
But

no matter how hard I stare, I can't see the other side
so today can't be crossed.
Wandering like this, can I say that I've lived?

Is it all right if I don't live again?

Today, I think about washing my hair
so as not to leave irksome work for others when I die.
Ah, I'll have to vacate this room.
I must donate some books to the municipal library
burn diary and letters, take my leave. Goodbye.
What else?

To a today that can't stop today from happening
the term "natural death" must seem beautiful.

Like
something
only possible for things that fly without wings.

Like the heart?
For example
love and sorrow and anger.

If they are gravity
will the stones I threw ever fall to the ground?
When will that moon fall to the ground?
Who

threw that great stone?
The stone

flies through some uncharted today
and then finally forgetting what love is
forgetting what sorrow is, what anger is

if that stone turns into falling rain
and I get soaked

when I feel the pain
I finally understand
there is a god inside me as well.

I'm flooded
because death carries the flood of our bodies into today
and then vanishes behind the door.

Beyond the window lies the night sky
still smashed by the stone I threw long ago.
Shutting my eyes
one day I saw. A crowd of snowmen swimming in the sea. One day
I saw the footprints they had left printed in the river. Like clouds'
tranquility and manure's liberation, like birds' rest and worms'
freedom, if ever I can cross "Today,"

I will secretly conceal my head inside thought.

BREATH, BODY, DREAM

A word suitable to inflate a doll

Air.

Left and right briefly diverge in the air I am walking through.
Then, looking back, they converge into a me that the air is staring at.
For a long while
we were locking each other up.

It was a formality, filling you with the air issuing from my body
or filling my body with the air issuing from you.
It was just like being in water full of the word "breath."

No matter how we walk, we could never pass one another.

If I looked, thinking it was to the left, it was to the right
or if I looked around, thinking it was not to the right,
it was not to the left.

About now

I wish you would remove me from your memories.
I wish you would empty me out and hang me up.

Releasing air into air.

Laundry
is white.

When I see white things, I think of children.
I think of a horizon where left and right have disappeared.
There seems to be nothing inside white things.

When a child was distended
and bloated, pulling the white horizon with a long arc
someone burst it, pop, with a sharp word and
we flopped down like laundry fallen to the floor.

THINGS THAT HAVE GONE BY

Objects, books, alarm clocks, and flowerpots all full of spurge
and the windows next to them and even the diverging curtains

eyeless things open eyes and look at me.

Mouthless things open mouths and speak.

Those things speak

until the carefree ripples
tossed onto the lake of blood in my body have all settled.

Until my body has pierced the darkness with red.

Until the darkness has all leaked out into my body.

From objects, chimneys, clouds, and the wind
I clearly met but never saw
and the heart forever seen

the eyes of eyeless things vanish
and the mouths of mouthless things vanish.

Things that see return to seeing places
and things that speak return to speaking places.

You vanish again from a world where you don't exist.

TUESDAY'S BIRTHDAY IS TUESDAY

It would be better if nobody gave time any water.
Until its water-barrel flanks became empty.
Until it, after speeding along, became thirsty

and it collapses.

I meet nobody on a Tuesday. Sometimes I visit my home town
tell my aged mother lies
and even though I return home rushing along night roads
like a rearview mirror where nothing remains
I always feel like I haven't met anybody.

On days when I dreamed
I used to get up
and sit vacantly amidst the darkness.
Were those days like desert islands?

Places no one had discovered.

No matter on which map you look, Tuesday is not marked.
On the opposite side someone is asking in a loud voice.
Which way must I go for Sunday to emerge?
I feel I've passed through there . . .
but I cannot say in which direction it lay

The image of an empty sea.

I can write letters.

It's raining.
Somewhere in the sky, someone is giving birth to wingless birds.
It's raining.
Someone is chopping up fish and tossing them away.
My window is the first to go to ruin, in invisible places
rivers go to ruin.
But what of the people?

They are invisible.

MOON AND SWORD

Moon and
sword
somehow they resemble each other.

I send a text message
saying that night is similar to the depths of a scabbard.
Into a scabbard that is stabbed countless times without ever being cut

a sword is entering.

It's bloodstained. My, just look at that star.
So pretty.

It's so pretty that in some country a painting of a sword was made
instead of a moon and hung on a tall flagpole.
A country where every morning people bleeding stood like ghosts
gazing at a dead child.

In truth, a scabbard was born already suffering.
Was born dead.

I asked a corpse born as a corpse: Does it hurt?
I saw a star in your body.

I asked night:

Does it hurt even though you're dead? I asked Mother.

And so there is always weeping somewhere in the night
and yet I write again.

The moon rises, and night sparkles at the bottom of a dark well
that someone threw a sword into.

Let's try to get along well.

THAT YEAR'S TIDINGS

On the altar to a drowned god, is water needed or fire? This is not a story about the white beard of a turtle or the flaming eyes of a sea lion. A story of melting fish to save water from ice and baking fish to save fish from water. Just as shedding tears is not a testimony that we have come to the sea, just as having said we are sleeping does not mean we cannot learn death, just as we cannot graduate from death, this is not a tale about faith or about life. But once the evening comes when eating is over and sorrow is over and only death is not over, when we fall into our own blood and drown, is that a water burial or is that cremation?

Sorrow had gone off somewhere. Like a quiet funeral procession.

We cannot say that it was fallen leaves.

Just that I understood that
everything that cannot be known stabs empty time
that what had been left behind were wounds called the body
that fixed on the thumbtack called the body

the soul cannot go flying off

and it is not the case that death clings to a single corpse.

RAIN MISBEHAVING

In order to salvage itself in weeping, sorrow releases tears.
It's that deep
I, a misbehaving sea

that stretches my palm out of the window.

It doesn't mean that I regret it.
Because it started to rain

if I quietly turn and wipe the gleams faintly appearing above water
shadows with a dry towel

red bugs that have come seething over the body's floor
nibble away at the eyes beneath the eyelids.

Sorrow makes use of the whole of a landscape.

ICE MELTS WHILE BREAKING

All the stones in the world were once gravestones
or will become gravestones.

They say there is fire that melts stone but

since the letters that time carried off will be engraved on the wind
I believe that their lives frequented by my breath haven't yet ended.

Like the rising cold yellow moon dragging off every dark window
like dragging the solitary night away into that light's darkness

shadows of vanished time.
Death,
sorrow,
anger.

In the darkness, humans are always being broken.
Like youth coming to me hastily as if it did not know this life's seasons

on that room's windowpane are traces of a flying stone.
There is rejected solitude.

Winter rises white, capsizing ships.

But now is no time to cut time's stomach. Ultimately all fish drown.

Solitude can only be undissected.

When I cut a hand wiping a broken window
like blood vessels rising as earthquakes in the eye
becoming night after retreating into the background.

Now is the single night of a moon
someone has thrown after crumpling it up.

When I take a step forward, humanity moves.

When I take a step forward
crumbs called fog, and
a huge, white rock can be seen rolling slowly into time's ravine.

I have heard that somewhere in this world
there is a vast cemetery for the drowned that is called the sea.

A body slowly pours in.

FULL-SCALE LIFE

Here is like the inside of the body of an atheist
who has attended his lover's funeral.
Sorrow rises on a large scale.

The entrance is always open.
Go *rushing in.*
The street is the chapel of those unable to pray.
Cha—pel.
There was someone who said he grew sad
if he pronounced those syllables
the baptismal name attached to faith without prayer.

The sorrow that sits in a circle inside his mouth is pressed meat
thrown it into a dark cavern.

Who is that piling up tongues flat on the altar of night
lacquered with crows' cawing?
Who is that person wriggling white?
Is there a floor
here, too?

Echoing hollow, a voice replied.

Who is it?
Who is it?
Is it?

And yet it is. Here chicken meat threaded onto skewers cooks
cowhide is being fixed on a handle
and people carrying candles walk wearing masks.
Once past this street

raising cross-shaped scissors and cutting black hair
all night, the chapel stands
it's great mouth gaping.

Here is the exit for the words going in.

Chopping up sorrow as pressed meat
go rushing in.

For the worship of those unable to pray
some candles bear the print of shoes

PARTING

Descending at Yongsan station, I saw it. To the bitter end, on the rails, a train that didn't descend.

BEFORE I COLLAPSED AND DREAMED

Intent on peeping into life, death sowed love in people.
It grew up as a double agent.

I am inserting the gods' plug once more.

In order to communicate my fury — *if you have any disasters left for me*
I hope you send them before midnight.

ABOUT THE AUTHOR:

Born in Geochang, South Gyeongsang Province, Korea, in 1974, Sin Yong-Mok received a new writers award in 2000 and has published six collections of poetry, a volume of prose essays, and a novel. He received several awards for his work prior to the collection When Someone Called Someone I Looked Back (2017), which received the 2017 Baek Seok Award for Poetry. He is currently a professor in the Creative Writing Department of Chosun University, Gwangju, South Jeolla Province.

ABOUT THE TRANSLATOR:

Brother Anthony has lived in Korea since 1980 and has published some fifty volumes of English translations of contemporary Korean poetry in addition to a considerable number of translations of Korean fiction, and other books related to Korea. He is an emeritus professor at Sogang University, a chair professor at Dankook University, and President Emeritus of the Royal Asiatic Society Korea Branch.

ABOUT THE SERIES

The Moon Country Korean Poetry Series publishes new English translations of contemporary Korean poetry by both mid-career and up-and-coming poets who debuted after the IMF crisis. By introducing work which comes out of our shared milieu, this series not only aims to widen the field of contemporary Korean poetry available in English translation, but also to challenge orientalist, neo-colonial, and national literature discourses. Our hope is that readers will inhabit these books as bodies of experience rather than view them as objects of knowledge, that they will allow themselves to be altered by them, and emerge from the page with eyes that seem to see "a world that belongs to another star."